DATE DUE

| | |
|---|---|
| JUN 16 1993 | |
| JUL 2 1993 | |
| DEC 23 1993 | |
| MAR 23 1994 | |
| JAN 23 1995 | |
| FEB - 6 1995 | |
| FEB 20 1995 | |
| JAN 18 1996 | |
| FEB 13 1996 | |
| Feb 27 | |
| MAR 19 1996 | |
| APR 29 1996 | |
| JAN 25 1997 | |
| APR 30 1997 | |
| JAN 29 1999 | |
| | |
| | |
| | |
| | |

# The Meanings of Modern Design

PETER DORMER

# The Meanings of Modern Design

## TOWARDS THE TWENTY-FIRST CENTURY

With 50 illustrations

THAMES AND HUDSON

The publishers would like to thank Design Analysis International for their help in producing this book.

First published in the United States in 1990 by Thames and Hudson Inc., 500 Fifth Avenue, New York, New York 10110

Library of Congress Catalog Card Number 89-51583

Printed and bound in Great Britain

# CONTENTS

*Paul Storey*, A Vision, *1987*.

# Preface

Why do we buy so many things? Who persuades designers to restyle everything continuously? Consumer, manufacturer, advertiser? Or the designers themselves? Why and in what ways do art, craft, handicraft and hand finishing have relevance to design in an industrialized consumer culture?

While it is not always the case, underpinning the huge contemporary interest in designed objects is the apparent truth that, given the opportunity, people like acquiring things. Their (our) desire for possessions accounts for the success of manufacturing industry and design. Perhaps there are *subtle* reasons to explain the varieties of acquisitiveness, but there are also plain ones: washing machines and other tools make life easier (and to that extent pleasanter); other things, such as chairs, provide comfort; and there are objects of distraction, such as radios, hi fi, television and toys. There are also objects, some of which are categorized as art, others as craft, that we want around us to lend colour, variety or expression to life.

Few of these things are necessary for brute survival. But since the increase of our populations and the complexity of our social relations have gone hand-in-hand with developments in energy production, medicine and commerce, it could be argued that we depend for our very existence on what some people argue is an excess. The elaborations of modern material culture are such that we are like the myriad insects of the rain forest, mutually interdependent upon a complex, seemingly wasteful, byzantine collection of relations and conditions. *Brute* survival, in the sense of our becoming nomads foraging for food, is not even a possibility.

Nevertheless, what makes designers, manufacturers and their objects irresistibly interesting is that they work at the heart of materialist cultures; they work where expression can be given to a variety of cultural achievements and human aspirations. In this book the emphasis is upon the designer as stylist – as a broker of ideas and values, a middle personage between the manufacturers, engineers and applied scientists on the one hand, and the consumer on the other.

All supportive relationships must possess shared values. If the manufacturer is to make a profit, if the designer is to earn a fee, and if the consumer's self esteem is to be raised, then everybody must share a language. There have to be agreements about what looks good, about what materials are to be valued and why they are valued; there has to be a shared view of what is worth aspiring towards, and how aspirations can be reinforced with material goods. These agreements are present in the conventions of taste, class and fashion that characterize a culture at any given point of its history.

Consequently, the possibility of an *avant garde* in design is more restricted than it is in fine art – this is obvious, for, if design moves too far ahead of what people understand, then it fails them as consumers and they stop consuming. In contemporary fine art, the idea that many people should catch up the *avant garde* is no longer regarded as important; as a result, the majority of people ignore it.

There are important differences between the economic framework within which art, as opposed to design, generally operates, but the economic structure and the ambitions of artists and designers do sometimes overlap in high design and fine craft. High design and craft are both areas in which exclusivity is a commodity and where high prices are charged for objects whose aesthetic value may only be recognizable to the cognoscenti. An extreme example of this was the furniture produced by the Memphis group of Milan in the early 1980s. This work had no popular appeal, nor is it clear that it was intended to. Museums have bought it as a cultural phenomenon and a few wealthy collectors have followed suit.

In general, designers and manufacturers cannot afford to be too much in front of their consumers' tastes, or – in an era of growing ecological consciousness – their concerns. But this does not mean that the consumer provides all the influences upon a designer or a manufacturer. The manufacturer and the designer experiment and entice and try out new things that no consumer ever asked for, or even expected. To whet the appetite of potential consumers the manufacturer relies upon the services of professional enticers – the advertising agencies. Advertisers help to make the values that shape consumerism.

How this relationship works is hard to pin down. The different elements – design, consumerism and the image making of consumerism created through advertising – are fluidly related: the process is continuous, like putting coloured oils on the surface of the water and watching them mix and swirl. Sometimes you can see where one colour touches another, sometimes the boundary is impossible to define. The coloured oils of materialism are added to by television advertising, design and consumer magazines.

All design involves the expression of values, whether overtly or covertly, but the categories of object that this book examines are:

1   Consumer durables – such as hairdryers, electric kettles, vacuum cleaners

2   Craft – handmade pots, furniture, textiles, jewelry

3   High design artefacts – artefacts that can include a lot of handworkmanship (expensive cars, watches and tea services are included), but that are designed by people who do not make them: named architects or star designers.

The book's structure reflects the importance of four themes – the economic context for all design and production, including that of handcrafted manufacture; the role that new technology appears to be playing in changing the possibilities for stylists; the relationship between making, consuming and individual self-satisfaction; and the increasing need to set design in the context of society's larger values – towards health and safety, individual job satisfaction and responsibilities for the environment. The book does not, therefore, take its cue from the histories of individual designers.

Our late twentieth-century relationship with consumerism is, however, equivocal. For, while we recognize the success and the pleasures made possible by the culture of consumerism, the current spiral of excess cannot continue without national and pan-national frameworks to govern the manufacture of the things we consume. Currently, we are putting the earth under too much pressure: we are in genuine danger of poisoning it. And the 'we' that is reponsible applies largely to the West and Japan. The rest of the world has yet to join the consumers' club.

*Designing Style*, my first chapter, sets out the territory for the rest of the book and explains the distinction between 'below' and 'above the line' via which design as style has been separated from design as engineering. In Chapter Two, *Ninety Years On*, the broad economic context for changing styles in 20th-century design is established, with a particular emphasis upon the importance of the American economy and foreign policy.

One of the assumptions often and understandably made is that war is the great engine of innovation and design advance. Chapter Three, *As Water Is In Water*, indicates that much has in fact been done in peace through the engine of consumerism itself, although helped to some extent by the defence and aerospace industries, supported – as in war – by taxation rather than profit-led commerce. Chapter Three focuses, however, on the effects of new materials upon styling.

*Our Domestic Landscape* (Chapter Four) looks first at the design and styling of tools and then at 'pseudo-tools' – thus washing machines are considered as a 'real' tool, while the hobbyist's 35 mm SLR camera, with all its add-ons, is looked at as a pseudo-tool. The chapter then goes on to discuss the role of symbolism and meaning in product style – issues that recur in different forms in subsequent chapters. Thus, in Chapter Five, *High Design* examines the role of symbolism in marketing to the rich or the 'wish-they-were-rich', placing importance on the role of handcraftsmanship in this sector.

Handcraftsmanship in the role of the studio crafts is the main theme of Chapter Six, *Valuing the Handmade* – the thesis is advanced that contemporary crafts are a 20th-century invention and gain their meaning not only through their opposition to design and industry but also through their separation from the ethic of price competitiveness.

The final chapter, *Design Futures*, argues for a conservationist and a conservative approach to design. Just as consumers have succeeded in securing for themselves a plenitude of things, the next logical extension of consumerism (which is happening before our eyes) is concern for the environment. And as the 20th century reaches its end, it is also worth observing that while in design, as in all other activities, there is a place for scepticism, even the hardest sceptic has to head for the warm sea of belief if he or she is to find what makes any kind of life tolerable – innate values.

# 1

# DESIGNING STYLE

## The Relationship between Style and Engineering

*Above the line and below it*

In some government circles there are references to 'above the line' or 'below the line' discussions. 'Above the line' is for public discussion, 'below the line' is not. The doctrine is literally applied: on a printed agenda, a line is ruled; the items listed beneath that line are secret and are to be kept hidden.

In the military world, for example, there is always much that is 'below the line'. For a long time the California-based Northrop aerospace company was not making the radar-avoiding *Stealth* bomber for the US Government, which in turn had not commissioned its manufacture, despite the fact that leading Washington reporters said that it was and that it had.

In domestic design, there is also an 'above' and a 'below the line' distinction. This has less to do with secrecy than with what it is thought the consumer wants to see and understand in his or her home. There are, of course, many differences between styling and engineering. One of the more important relates to the extent that a consumer needs to be cajoled into a purchase. For example, with medical equipment – say for research into animal and human physiology – there is no need for the engineer and manufacturer to disguise or package the equipment prettily. To a layperson much of the apparatus, especially the devices for restraining animals, looks quite appalling. But those who practise with such apparatus are (a) attuned to the purpose and (b) not interested in what it looks like, but in how it performs.

The factory workplace is another area where there is less demand for the functionalist attributes to be softened in their appearance. But the closer one gets to the public or to the home, the greater the need for the

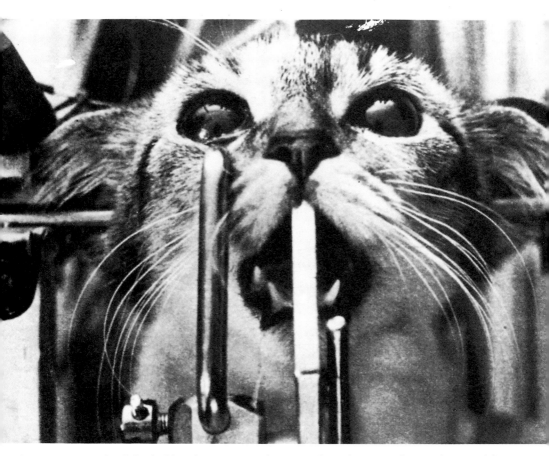

*Much of the hidden design in our lives involves the pain of animals. But debate is hampered by animal rights terrorism, which has made animal exploiters even more secretive.*

stylist to intercede with a repertoire of visual good manners. There is thus a distinction between the stylist and the engineer. The stylists have been more clamorous in public, the engineers remain largely anonymous. Occasionally, an engineer will become famous – but not so often as a stylist. Consequently, in the public's eye designers = stylists.

One reason why stylists are becoming stars and engineers and applied scientists remain anonymous is that the latter are not always identifiable: how many scientists or engineers can be said to have contributed towards a television set or a personal computer? By contrast, a single stylist can draw a line around the communal and complicated efforts of the engineering input and present a single, unified image to the world of the consumer.

'Below the line' design is the design that the consumer does not see – either because the design is literally out of sight, as in the molecular engineering that produces new synthetic materials, or because it refers to components that make the object work but that do not *visibly* add value to the product. 'Below the line' design is usually the most important because it determines how well the object functions – but only rarely is this province drawn attention to in the attempt to attract the consumer. Sometimes second-order objects or 'distress purchases' are made attractive by advertisers, who cleverly draw attention to the ingenuity of the science possessed by such things as radio batteries and automobile engine oil. For example, in seeking to make one particular brand of engine oil an attractive buy, the advertising agency drew attention and perhaps glamour to the invisible science of motor oil by calling it 'liquid engineering'.

Nevertheless, consumers usually and understandably ignore 'below the line' design until there is a failure. 'Below the line' design fails for any or all of three reasons: insufficient knowledge by the manufacturer or designer; carelessness in construction; or the end of the natural life of the component. The criteria for success or failure in 'below the line' and second-order design are sometimes horribly clear cut – parts fail, people die. The order and nature of responsibility of design at the second and hidden layers are generally fundamental and can physically affect human and animal life or the environment.

The *Challenger* shuttle is a recent example. Partly for political reasons (the public had to be convinced that public funds should be spent on Space to the profit of private industrialists) and partly because extending ourselves into the solar system is exciting and conceptually invigorating, NASA has over the years kept the after-burners lit on its publicity machine by asserting that in 'below the line' design it has been consistent in obtaining good quality. American space technology was itself a metaphor for the best in design.

Naturally public imagination – my imagination – was intrigued by the more stylish and visible elements of the minutiae that made up the programme – the spacemen's boots, backpacks and internal spacecraft controls. The imagination was not troubled by things like rubber ring seals, nor even those heat-shielding ceramic tiles that kept coming loose like roof tiles in the wind. Who, except a plumber, is excited by the design of the pipes in their own home?

The *Challenger* space shuttle explosion caused as great a rupture in the Western consumer's imagination as the collapse of the Tay Bridge in Victorian Britain. Building a bridge then, building a space shuttle now, are examples of the pinnacles of material achievement – sudden collapse causes a sudden deflation in the consumer's faith in design and, temporarily, in the culture in which he or she has a role. Moreover, although such achievements are or were seen as pinnacles, they were also taken for granted and assumed to be safe.

The layperson's faith is also fed by the elaborations of contemporary stories, myths and metaphors. Space exploration in particular has been accompanied by some virtuoso extended metaphors to feed our imagination. Consider *2001 A Space Odyssey*, which celebrated the superior technology of American culture. The film presented, as a 'reality', space as a stainless enterprise in which the normal errors of human endeavour had been removed – what went wrong in the world of Kubrick's fiction was the waywardness of another but non-human intelligence, namely that of HAL, the exasperating intelligent computer who spoke in the voice of a Mormon missionary.

Of course, national chauvinism affects the way we see design: think, for example, of the way in which the Chernobyl nuclear power station disaster was reported and discussed in the West. The explosion was generally accepted by Westerners as a peculiarly Russian incident because it is assumed that Russian technology is always inferior to North American or West European. Some of this chauvinism may have to do with styling – to Western eyes, or at least to my eyes, Russian design often looks lumpen and utilitarian, to the extent that it implies that the 'below the line' design is still immature and vulnerable to sudden breakdown. In part the lumpiness in Russian space design is the result of 'below the line' design in electronics – Russian technology has not got so far with the development of microprocessors as Western. It is probable that, had a Russian space ship exploded, the Western faith in design and technology in the space field would have been barely dented. Our assumptions about the superiority of Western technology are probably not overly justified. Oddly styled or not, the Soviet space craft perform well.

But 'below the line' technology – because it is 'below the line' – can keep its worse aspects hidden, and among its worst aspects are sloppy procedures. The science might be pure, but the application is sometimes too human in its fallibility. When the *Challenger* blew up it was a shock, but the biggest shock was in learning that NASA's vulnerability lies in the crudity, as much as the refinement, of space technology – technology in which we had trusted.

Nevertheless, the popular, general and to some extent well-founded image of the nature of science and technology is that there is no *trial and error* in modern Western technology once a thing has gone into the production stage or the stage where human life or formidable expense is involved. Prototype aircraft, for example, are not expected to crash even if they are being flight-tested for the first time. A lot of bench testing and computer modelling precedes the launch of expensive hardware. It is also bad publicity if a commercial airliner, for example, crashes – even as a prototype.

Laypeople are also reassured by the belief that, if an engineer uses something, then a scientist behind him or her understands how and why it works. This faith is, on the whole, justified, but trial and error have not left 'below the line' design entirely. Sometimes we have to use materials that do a job well before we know why they do their job well.

In the last thirty years our faith in technology has grown enormously because several visible technologies have matured into sophistication and reliability – automobiles and aircraft are two examples. After a spate of aircraft crashes there is no substantial falling off of people willing to fly.

There will be other references to 'below the line' design in this book, but it is worth summarizing the features of the relationship between product engineering, product styling and the consumer.

1   'Below the line' design and its responsibilities are too complicated, too numerous and frequently too arcane to interest the lay consumer. Some people argue that design and engineering are often intrinsically too complicated for an individual to understand them. No one person *knows* the totality of a Boeing 747.

2   Given the truth of (1), it is also true that the lay consumer likes the occasional reassurance that all is well under the styling and/or that what is being bought is state-of-the-art technology.

3   The connection between (1) and (2) is expressed in part by the

designer as stylist and in part by the advertiser. Both the stylist and the advertiser work to increase the general metaphor of a product's invincibility and inherent goodness. On the whole, the worlds of activity that go into the production of objects are kept separate from a product's style. There is little to be gained *commercially* in reminding people of the unpleasantness or uncertainties that can undermine manufacturing.

Consider, for example, the case of Boeing and Japan Airlines (JAL). The Boeing 747 Jumbo jet is regarded by many people, including the author, as a very safe aircraft to travel in. But one of JAL's 747s did crash and the loss of life was appalling; the cause, apparently, was a faultily repaired bulkhead which, despite stringent checking, had a flaw that was not detected. However, there was no reason – and there is no reason – to doubt the safety of 747s generally (the circumstances under which the fated JAL airliner came to be repaired were very special). JAL, at the time of writing this (1988–89) is buying more 747s and the Japanese press is running stories about faults in newly delivered 747s. The faults have been relatively minor. Indeed, in normal circumstances these small and easily corrected flaws (such as a fire extinguisher hung upside down) would have been too boring for a newspaper, especially as the airline de-snags its aircraft before putting them into service. But an unusual conjunction of events meant a sudden and widespread interest in the 'below the line' design of the 747. These events included not only the crash in 1985 of the JAL airliner, but a labour dispute within JAL itself such that, in order to make life difficult for the company, disgruntled employees have been telephoning the newspapers every time a flaw, however small, has been detected. JAL's response has been typically thorough in a Japanese way: it has introduced a system of maintenance and checking whereby a team of specialists is allocated to each aircraft for the rest of the aircraft's life.

In 1989, following incidents and a crash (in Britain) involving Boeing aircraft (not 747s), the aviation authorities in the USA and Britain ordered special wiring checks on new Boeings. Faults were found. What is surprising is not that faults were found, but that the world expects their total elimination. Of course, manufacturers and service industries must aim for perfection, but they and we, as the consumers, make mistakes more rather than less likely by believing in the myths of technology, rather than in what common sense and common experience should teach us. To demand perfection is sensible; to expect it can be fatal.

## Nice styles

Styling is the visual language that says to a culture that it is ordering itself successfully into productive patterns of work, leisure and institutions. Ordering affairs ensures not only that a culture can continue but that it will enlarge and progress. Even so simple a styling device as tidiness is often as much a visual declaration of intent as it is a necessary feature for what is tidied to function. People who are uncertain as to their power over their bit of world sometimes become obsessive in their tidiness – a neat terrain, an over-ordered nation or merely the dust swept beneath the carpet reassure us that we are still in control.

At the time this book is being written the ruling philosophy in styling among the vocal young designers is called 'reacting against the black box aesthetic' – an archetype of the 'tidying-up aesthetic'.

From the early 1950s through to the 1970s, there had been a successful fashion among some designers and some manufacturers for putting the mechanical or large electrical components of hairdryers, radios, electric shavers, stereo systems, televisions and video players inside smooth black, grey or white plastic cases. The shape and form of these cases were geometric: boxes, cylinders and, occasionally, spheres. The prevalence of the style, especially in electrical goods, coincided with a similar style in architecture.

An elegant art historical pedigree for 'black boxes' runs from the 19th-century painter Paul Cézanne (considered to be a father of modernism), via Johannes Itten (one of this century's most influential art teachers at the Bauhaus), through to Braun, the West German manufacturer of domestic electrical goods.

But modernism has had both a bad press and a misleading one. It is now fashionable to mock the *form follows function* argument which held that an honest design did not attempt to disguise what it did, how it worked and even what it was made from and how it was constructed. Such design philosophy was once held to be honest and democratic; and given the political context of its most formative period – perhaps 1914 to around 1930 – it was appropriate for socialist and revolutionary politics. After all, if the politics were in opposition to established mores, the aesthetics had to be in opposition also.

However, *form follows function* was only a style. The argument that modernist design took its cue from the logic of mass manufacturing was not true (see pp.145–6). If the dominant style of the objects and architecture produced by the old, non-socialist establishment had been plain and functional, then I am sure that the aesthetic riposte of the socialist or democratically inclined designers would have been towards elaboration, figuration and decoration. The point is that you can argue either style both ways: both can be seen as oppressive, both can be seen as democratic. You can say that you are being honest about the object's role, or that you are bringing decoration and metaphor to the people. You can almost toss a coin.

What remains true is that either approach – the formal or the elaborated – has an aesthetic integrity independent of the ideology adopting it. Moreover, this integrity can be violated. And the integrity of modernism was violated after the Second World War – modernism was turned into brutalism, and second-rate cheapskate utilitarianism.

By the late 1970s, those who felt boxed in themselves, began to assert that the black box/white cylinder aesthetic was bland, anonymous and too generalized. Electrical domestic goods in particular were seen as 'lacking individuality'. This lack of individuality was rooted in the practicalities of manufacture – they were relatively simple forms to produce. There were also other factors that led to the success of the simple aesthetic: domestic artefacts, such as food mixers or blenders or coffee grinders or weighing machines, are bound to be regarded first as tools, not ornament. Nevertheless, some tools are by their nature more individual and 'expressive' than others. For example, a hammer is unequivocal in expressing what it does best: bashing things. But some modern tools do not overtly express their function. A modern styled-up domestic weighing machine for the kitchen does not *express* weighing; it is just a little dais on which you place a plastic bowl with your flour or butter within it, and read off the weight through a little window beneath which are liquid crystal digital figures.

However, an old-fashioned set of kitchen scales expresses the act of weighing a quantity whose weight is unknown against a set of standard weights. It is as expressive as trying to weigh two things relative to one another using just one's hands. With the old machine one knew what

The crustacean sculpture by Ann Carrington (UK, 1987) draws attention to the metaphorical richness of basic kitchen tools — a richness which some of today's designers are seeking to create in their own work.

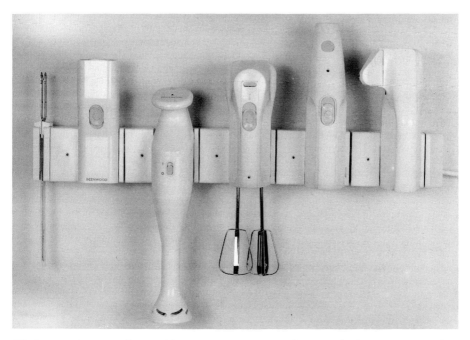

Kitchen equipment, designed by Pentagram (UK) for Kenwood (UK). Beautiful? Expressionless? Unnecessary? Why use polluting energy (electricity) when muscle power will suffice? That, surely, depends on whose muscles are involved.

weighing *felt* like. But the modern tool is probably more accurate, convenient and hygienic – as well as beautiful in its own right.

Black box design allegedly caused consumers to feel excluded. A black box looks like sorcery; it does not reveal how it functions. The attitude this style can be said to express parallels the attitudes of paternalistic professionalism in Western society: architects, lawyers, doctors and others do things to you rather than with you. On the other hand it appears to be true that most people most of the time want to be spared the details of the 'below the line' design in the service they are buying – whether it is surgery or stereo equipment.

At the moment there is a swing towards stylistic individuality. This may be ironic in relation to the 'below the line' developments in Western society, which are towards globalism and corporatism, and the 'above the line' advertising that has made Coca-Cola, Pepsi-Cola, Macdonalds, or American Express known to everyone from Colorado to Calcutta. Among designers there is a fashion for persuading manufacturers that individualism, niche marketing, niche design and serving minority interests should become the rule. Manufacturers become interested in niche marketing if it can be made more profitable than 'mass' marketing.

David Pye, writer, designer and craftsman, clarifies the nature of fashion in design in his book *The Nature and Aesthetics of Design* (1974). The young generation grows up under the 'restraints, or imagined restraints' imposed by the older generation which mothered and fathered it. Inevitably the style of the older generation is associated by the younger with 'restraint'. The style of the older generation is rejected. But soon the younger generation has begat a generation of its own, a similar process of association and rejection occurs, and then the newest generation rediscovers the quality of its grandfather's generation.

Simple. Too simple, as David Pye himself says. But there is some truth in his observation. Moreover, although Pye does not say this, the *passion* with which one generation rejects a style in order to argue for its own, is a guarantee of that style possessing its own integrity. Terms like 'fashion' and 'style' are too easily dismissed as referring to things that are superficial because they are ephemeral. We should not lose sight of the fact that change is as much a sign of constant inquiry, searching, innovation and speculation as it is also a sign of opportunism.

Modernism had a design integrity which will be re-discovered just as, miraculously, people are now celebrating the design achievements of work done in the 1950s and the 1890s. What Pye describes is another aspect of the phenomenon of the emotion of nostalgia and our willingness to look back. Time literally puts things in perspective, but there are other reasons why designers as stylists find it easier to applaud a style that is at least a generation removed from that of their parents. Ambitious designers and artists find it easier to praise the virtues of those who are either retired, dead or generally perceived as *hors de combat*. Parents and teachers are seldom *hors de combat*.

Does the rejection of modernism have a special edge to it that previous rejections have lacked?

Some commentators have remarked on an apparent lack of humanity in the work of one of modernism's major figures – Le Corbusier, architect, painter and designer. This apparent lack of humanity stemmed in part from the fact that Le Corbusier's style did not transfer very easily from one region of the world to another. (Nor did many of his buildings have enough figurative content for the individual to relate to, his pilgrimage church of Notre Dame-du-Haut being an exception.)

Lack of humanity in modernist architecture, together with its ubiquity (whole cities were transformed), impelled a popular backlash against the style. And popular, as opposed to professional and partisan rebellions, are quite rare in architecture and design.

There has not been a popular or widespread outspokenness against the black box aesthetic in product design (except for some designers, it hardly seems to be an issue at all). Some consumers may have become bored with the style; others, on the Pye Principle, may associate it too much with their childhood. But, whereas modernist architecture did transform the lives of millions of people, black box aesthetics did not. In the majority of homes in which black box stereo units or televisions were or are to be found, it is probable that there will also be found comfortable, blousy soft furnishings, fitted carpets, Scandinavian-style dining suites or reproductions of some sort. Black box in design did not have the ubiquity of glass box architecture. It is misleading to overstate the dominance of one design style over another in Western capitalist society. It is true that black box held sway in a category of goods – electrical – but a home contains a variety of objects and, consequently, a variety of styles.

With new materials (see Chapter Three) have come new freedoms for stylists. There is a marketing-led emphasis upon user-friendliness, lightness, perceived safety, and narrative content. Designers and manufacturers have microcircuitry and the freedom to use electronic rather than electro-mechanical devices.

The effect of this freedom of style granted by materials science on mainstream design is discussed in Chapter Four, but some interesting, innovative work in what might be called 'narrative' design is emerging from the United States. The architects Michael Graves and Robert Venturi have been most influential in laying down a groundwork for this style and among the new generation to thrive in the atmosphere of expressiveness are the graduates of the Cranbrook school of product semantics.

The idea of 'narrative' in design requires closer investigation. American 'popular' taste of the early 1950s, as revealed by the domestic design of the period, produces parallels with developments in the late 1980s. (It is of interest that Helen Drutt, gallery owner, collector and critic, maintains that the much-lauded Memphis style was an intellectual highjacking of American 1950s homestyle.) There is a house in Philadelphia with a collection of 1950s artefacts that would have made Andy Warhol blench with envy. Cookie jars, TV lamps, curtains, table cloths, pinafores, clocks, chairs, lunch boxes and condiment sets have been gathered together in an unassuming row house by two astute collectors. All the objects are figurative, colourful, mass produced and cheap. We see clocks in the form of TVs or teapots, a radio in the form of a Firestone sparking plug, TV lamps in the form of animals and ballet dancers, or even constructed as Virgin Mary grottos. There are condiment sets in which the salt is a nude recumbent woman and the pepper is a nude recumbent man. Every flat surface, whether kitchen table (plastic top and chromed legs) or side of a paper napkin dispenser is embellished with pattern, sometimes abstract but more often of figures or plants or animals. There is a continuous demonstration of the art of making one object suggest another.

The narrative is sometimes very specific – a lunch box done up like a loaf of bread – but often more general. Much of the decoration of the textiles, for example, is quasi-ethnic and depicts happy Mexicans, or happy black mamas, or happy non-whites of some sort. There are references to film and TV characters. The context of these little narrations

*Sparking plug radio (USA) – a plastic sparking plug functioning as a transistor radio. This promotional gift has an on/off switch and tuner at the top.*

is a much bigger narration: advertising – and the substructures upon which advertising is built, from cinema and films to TV and radio, all of which provided further images that are reflected in the designs. The TV lamps of the period are fascinating in that (a) the television was the focal point of the room, therefore the TV lamp was an artefact of great importance; and (b) the lamp was an opportunity for a utilitarian work of domestic art in which the exotic, the decorative and, quite often, the religious were brought together. Consequently, it presented a very generalized summary of taste, dream and belief. Not bad for a lamp. I do not like these lamps and would not, Andy Warhol and his cookie jars notwithstanding, want to collect them. But their importance as ornament with meaning in the homes of ordinary intelligent people was such that I would be hesitant about mocking them.

*Popular design in the USA was designated 'naïve' when it was seen as working-class taste (these examples c. 1951). Then the plastic narrative attitude became respectable as 'post-modernism', wrought by the minds of star designers such as Michael Graves. (Opposite) His famous tea kettle with the plastic singing-bird spout (Alessi, 1986).*

In fine-art history America may be famous for its abstractionists of the 1940s and 1950s, but a more consistent thread in the wider visual culture is a love for visual puns, figuration, verisimilitude and illusion. Whether we look at the cookie jar culture of working-class domestic taste, Disney World, the breadth of crafts and decorative arts, or the sculpture in the post-modern AT&T building in New York, we see a taste for literalness of expression.

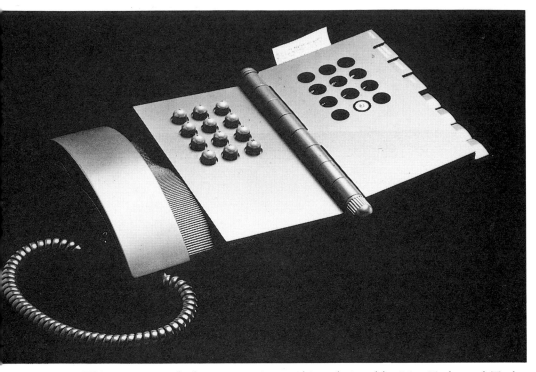

*This prototype telephone answering machine, designed by Lisa Krohn and Tucker Viemeister (USA, 1987), uses the simile of the book to make the machine friendly. American narratives again.*

There is a connection between a clock in the form of a teapot (*Tea Time*) and the telephone answering machine by Lisa Krohn and Tucker Viemeister designed in the form of a book – and this is not to belittle Krohn's work, nor to underestimate her understanding of what she is doing. Of her award-winning answering machine, she says: 'An integrated phone and answering machine, the Phonebook employs simile as both an appearance icon and a guide to its operation. Rigid plastic pages are turned to pass from the mode of making calls to recording and replaying or printing messages, just as flipping through a personal agenda turns up its different uses. In a way, Phonebook was a sugar coating on the pill of technology.'

By making the comparison between a contemporary serious design and what many will dismiss as merely Fifties kitsch I am drawing attention to the rich vein of popular demand for narrative design.

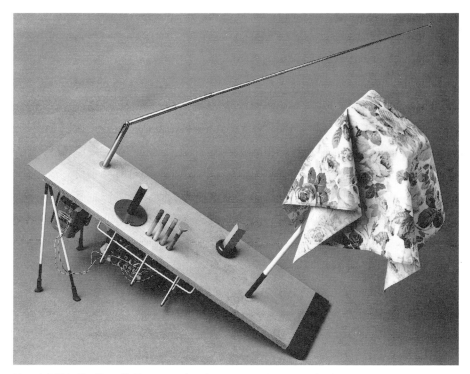

*Daniel Weil's* Small Door *radio (UK, 1986) is a multi-layered conceit. Weil, a foreigner in London, was hugely amused at the industrial backwardness of England's manufacturing industry.*

A different approach to narrative design, more subversive and, as it happened, uncommercial, is provided by Daniel Weil's *Small Door* radio. Weil is an Argentinian Jew who has worked extensively in Italy and has a design practice in London. *Small Door* is an oblique look at British taste and the old-fashionedness of domestic Britain. The guts of the radio hang beneath the wooden platform – the radio guts come from a Roberts radio, and Roberts radios were renowned for their solidity, good quality and boring design. The big plastic switches, with their candy-coloured stripes, recall small British confectionary shops selling sweets (candies) of dubious content made by tiny firms in the black heart of Britain's industrial belt. The crazy positioning of the speaker (on a pole) is covered up with a piece of chintz – covering things that are ugly with a rampant decorative textile is a time-honoured lower-middle-class expediency throughout the Western world. Weil's radio is more allusive and elusive than Krohn's answering machine. Krohn has an object that is clear in its vocabulary and therefore will be understood by a lot of people very easily. Weil's radio causes much puzzlement, some ridicule, and some delight.

## *No autonomous artisans?*

Most of the success our culture enjoys is the result of people working together, of specialization and co-ordinated fragmentation of work. No single person could nurture the complexity of an advanced design on his or her own. This is obviously true of a Boeing 747, but it is also true of relatively small and unglamorous components such as the new breed of high-impact automobile bumpers.

And all of the more complicated, most valuable creations of modern society, whether these be the governmental and administrative processes of running services or the practicalities of manufacturing radios, videos, motor cars or plastic widgets, entail people working co-operatively on parts of the enterprise. Culture is a co-operative, cumulative venture.

The success of industrial cultures has produced some reaction against it. There is a need for us to believe that it is still possible to earn a living making things by hand, to one's own rhythm and with oneself being in command of the total process. Craftsmen and craftswomen may be considered as people who direct the whole of their work process as well as the design of their artefacts.

Whatever the achievements of the group approach, it appears that there is also a deep-rooted need to believe in the worth, the uniqueness and the capability of the individual. This need explains the popular interest in public demonstrations of manual and mental skills – such as the virtuoso performance of a violinist or a hand thrower on a potter's wheel. We like to see people doing clever things.

The 20th century has seen the creation of a myth about craftsmanship and the 20th century has also redefined, if not re-invented, a role for the craftsperson. The nature of both the myth and the new role is discussed in Chapter Six. But the great selling point of craftsmanship is the variety of its narrative content and this holds true whether the artefact is a handmade shirt, a luxury motor car or handthrown pot.

*Marta Rogoyska, tapestry weaver, at work. A craftsperson must love his or her material. A designer need not love any single medium. The essence of craft is working a particular material.*

For example, the way we see contemporary handmade pots is surely affected by the fact that the pot is a token of someone's way of work and way of life. One could say the same about buying a motor car: buy a car and you buy a token of several hundred persons' way of life – in a sense. But one of the differences that distinguishes the design-led and mass-manufactured object from the craft object, is that the one seeks to disguise the reality of its labour whilst the other seeks to celebrate it. No one wants to be reminded of the noise, the regulated shiftwork or the monotony underlined with resentment or even fear that are too often the characteristics of factory labour. A handbuilt pot, on the other hand, can afford to be open about its manufacture. There is no need for designers or advertisers or public relations persons to intervene between the potter and the pot.

When we buy handmade domestic pottery we are buying into a way of labour that people respect and even envy. In any case, one of the values of craft technology is that it is using a more accessible language: you can work out how a pot or a basket or a piece of cloth has been made

*The top of a Coca-Cola can is beautiful. An eighteenth-century metalsmith would have been excited by the accuracy and the fact that it is repeatable over and over again.*

and designed. You are let into the process even if you are hopeless at making things yourself. But with design-led objects for mass manufacture the process and the making is a mystery to most people. Most of us who are not designers would be hard put to explain the pedigree of a Cola tin.

The 'traditional' crafts provide a comforting metaphor in a world of perplexity. For them to do this they have also to take familiar forms. The continuing demand for traditional forms in pottery or furniture or tableware is the demand for familiarity – for a visual language that has roots. The great strength of the crafts rests in their common visual language of familiar shapes, forms and functions. It does not matter whether people actually want the teapots, jugs or bowls for use: what they are buying, first of all, is a general set of metaphors about the kind of labour that has produced them, the way of life that produces them and a visual language that is easily understood.

# 2

# NINETY YEARS ON

# Style in Design Since 1900

Western design is the way it is largely because of the liberal capitalist culture in which it exists and which it serves. Consequently a review of the 'history of design' in the West has to take account of the ideology underlying the recent history of consumerism. Design, like consumerism itself, is neither an amoral nor an apolitical activity.

In this survey much is elided, telescoped and otherwise condensed. It is clear, however, that to date design has been fueled by an ideology that rests on the concept of continuous growth. Continuous growth has, as an economic concept, become equated with the very notion of freedom itself. To buy as much as possible, as often as possible, is regarded as a right, a necessity almost. And it is an attitude from which design in the West has benefited. However, such an interpretation of freedom may itself become history. That is the subject of the first half of this chapter. The second half of the chapter conveys a brief analysis of changing styles in design.

## The right to choose

Design and designers owe their current eminence to the fact that they live in a capitalist and liberal society rather than, say, a Marxist–Leninist one. In so far as there are any true Marxist–Leninist nations, it appears that centrally planned directives have not encouraged consumerism (except perhaps as a reaction to shortages in basic goods) – and it is consumerism rather than the development of heavy industry that gives designers their 'creative' opportunity. The reason for this is simple: in the industrial setting a machine has only to do its job; it should be safe and easy to use, but it need not have a design that ingratiates itself with the user or cajoles the potential purchaser into buying it. In a centrally planned economy there is no need for a dozen marginally different types of machine when just two will satisfy necessity. There is no need for metaphorical or advertising-directed styling. Central planning probably does not encourage flair, *or* the 'unnecessary' elements of design.

Centralist planning probably also cuts down on technical innovation. For it appears that one of the successes of Western economic liberalism is its encouragement of technology and, possibly, the arts – artists are more or less free to explore whatever forms their fancy takes them.

However, the very freedoms enjoyed in the West may diminish both the effectiveness and the sharpness of the arts. In authoritarian countries the artist is often one of the key voices of opposition, and therefore art which challenges the official view is seized upon greedily, if only because it is different. In the West being different is being normal. It is arguable also that when the artist is in opposition to something, then his or her work has a subject matter, as well as the vigour of being different. Very often the art has to be of a subtle and metaphorical complexity such that it can avoid the philistine editing of the censor yet reveal to those who have ears and eyes an alternative vision. In recent times the films of the Russian Andrei Tarkovsky provide such an example.

Western-style consumerism did not, of course, start only after the Second World War or even this century. Simon Schama, in his *The Embarrassment of Riches*,[1] gives a convincing account of 17th-century Amsterdam in the full swing of a consumerist boom, with street after street of close-packed shops. Nevertheless, after the Second World War burgeoning consumption in the USA took design and consumption to new, vast levels of excess. The groundwork for this excess was laid down by the extraordinary performance of the leading participants. notably the USA, in the War itself.

After the Second World War built-in obsolescence became a built-in feature of the West's economy. Whether or not the experience of the war had an effect on the manufacturer and the designer's shared tolerance of built-in obsolescence is a moot point. Given the success of turning out weapons that were then subsequently destroyed, it is possible that this 'make 'n' destroy' attitude became an *idée fixe* in American manufacturing culture.

There was thus a belief in the ethics of spiralling consumption. This is the point that American design historian Kathryn B. Hiesinger makes in her excellent introductory essay for the *Design Since 1945* catalogue to the exhibition of the same title held at the Philadelphia Museum of Art in 1983. She writes: 'American industry identified *new* with *good* and defended planned obsolescence as sound economics: "The American consumer expects new and better products every year. He has become accustomed to the yearly automobile show . . . our custom of trading in our automobiles every year, of having a new refrigerator, vacuum cleaner or electric iron every three or four years is economically sound . . . It is truly an American habit, and it is soundly based on our economy of abundance."' Brave words quoted by Hiesinger from a book called *Design for Business* by J. Gordon Lippincott, published in 1947.

The belief that new was good was grounded in a belief in the virtue and the necessity of competition. It was not, in itself, a new belief, for it was well rooted in 19th-century entrepreneurialism and, in the USA, in early 20th-century business management theory and practice.

Competition in American liberal capitalism was not *laissez-faire*; it had a structure, an organization, an ideology and a *design*. All these elements were recognized and set down by F.A. Hayek, the Austrian-born economist and social scientist who published his now famous book *The Road to Serfdom* in 1944.

It was intended as a critique of socialist, especially Marxist–Leninist, central planning (Hayek argued it was almost bound to end in tyranny) and as an argument for capitalist liberalism. Hayek has, fairly regularly, been damned as much as he has been praised – and damned for being a fascist too, which is ironic given how strong an attack on fascism his book presents. His book was a colossal success in the United States and a lesser, more controversial success in Britain, which was understandable in view of the fact that the political orthodoxy there between 1945 and 1979 tended towards socialist ideals and central planning. Moreover, Britain, like several other West European countries, had established a form of welfare state which seemed then (and indeed now) to serve its peoples rather well. Thus Hayek's rigorous arguments against central or government planning seemed extreme when judged, for example, against a centrally planned national health service that seemed to work.

None the less, there is much that is appealing in Hayek's liberalism because he constantly stresses the non-desirability of putting decisions about how people should live into the hands of a few people. A consideration of public housing policies in many of the Eastern bloc countries, as well as in Britain and the USA, will reveal how disastrous and, indeed, tyrannical, centralized decision-making can be.

Hayek stated his position as follows:
1    'The liberal argument is in favour of making the best possible use of the forces of competition as a means of co-ordinating human efforts, not an argument for leaving things just as they are.'[2]
2    'In a competitive society the prices we have to pay for a thing, the rate at which we can get one thing for another, depend on the quantities of other things of which, by taking one, we deprive the other members of society. *This price is not determined by the conscious will of anybody.*' (My italics)[3]

Point one is extraordinarily perceptive and there exists a lot of empirical evidence to support it: consumerism, the designing and manufacturing of goods in competition with one another, has produced a variety of choice which clearly excites, entertains and satisfies the Western consumer. Taking automobiles alone, there is sufficient competition between Europeans, Japanese and Americans to provide a most extensive choice of transport. However, more perceptive still is the remark that competition comes through co-ordination and not a free-for-all. For anything more complicated than a handbuilt pot or a wicker basket, people have to come together to work, to design, to promote and to sell. It explains one of the phenomena that is pronounced in the USA, in Japan and Western Germany – that of big corporations competing hard against one another but each demanding of its employees a loyalty and a commitment to the company in an effort to make that company *best*.

Hayek will have known of the extensive research carried out in the USA – and, indeed, earlier in Germany – into how people can be encouraged to work together in order to compete with other groups of people working together.

One may observe that the Americans, like the Germans, have a talent for organization and rationalization. In 1911 an American, Frederick Winslow Taylor, published a book called *The Principles of Scientific Management*, aimed at making all work forces more efficient and in retrospect appearing to have had the effect of tuning the human being to the pace and the rhythms of the machines – whether conveyor belts or ranks of typewriters in an office. But companies and corporations soon found that this atomistic approach to labour, turning workers into separate parts of a human machine, needed tempering with better management methods because it was found that worker morale slumped, productivity was relatively weak and labour turnover high when the workers thought that they were regarded as *things* to be worked rather than as subjects to be worked with.

Other social scientists came to eminence. One of the classic practitioners of work study was George Elton Mayo, an Australian who emigrated to the USA and became head of the department of Industrial Research at Harvard in 1926. Before taking that post he had been called in to the Western Electric Company of Chicago to seek a solution to worker dissatisfaction and low productivity. He experimented with piecework, rest periods and free hot meals. Mayo established, and later developed as a science, the importance of managerial attitudes to fostering good working relationships. He later studied the importance of allowing people to work in natural groups and did much research into group psychology and the methods by which not only productivity but quality productivity could be encouraged.

Such 'below the line design' (contemporary designers like to think of design as a process and the design of management and worker morale fits that description) has been one of the factors enabling Western manufacturing industry to succeed in its goals for producing quality products. The work of Mayo, and others, contributed to the success of the capitalist liberal ethic of giving customers a genuine choice in what they bought.

Low morale sabotages quality; it makes 'the best' impossible to obtain.[4] In a competitive – as opposed to a centrally planned – economy the concept of 'best' is largely defined not by the producer but by the consumer. And, as the history of the post-Second World War consumer society seems to indicate, best is defined as being more than simply 'cheap'. 'Best' also includes value for money, reliability and service.

The result, as subsequent chapters note, has been the production of consumer durables that have a quality and a performance far beyond the ordinary requirements of the consumer. Cameras, motor cars, computers all perform at levels much higher than basic necessity. In non-liberal societies the individual is not free to choose what he or she wants, but must put up with the decision of a few planners as to what the individual is deemed to need. In all kinds of ways this seems to result in practice in a levelling down – in service, in quality, in design and in variety. The designer only comes into his or her own when his or her services are required to outbid a competitor in capturing the whim of the individual consumer. Spiralling consumption also means spiralling aspirations – consumption and aspiration feed off one another. It is small wonder that Eastern bloc authorities have kept secret from their workers those special shops for Party Members (where Western goods are for sale) and have blockaded Western magazines, films and video that portray Western goods. The censoring of aspiration is one approach to avoiding the censure of the populace. What you do not know, you do not seek.

The Second World War, in which all the producer nations did well in the increased production of weapons, was a great success for American planning (helped, of course, by the fact that no one was invading or bombing the American mainland). The statistics are extraordinary: in 1943–44 the Americans completed one ship every day and one aircraft every five minutes; the aeroplanes included the big, long-range bombers such as the Superfortress. The organization of factories and offices to co-ordinate this kind of production took the art of human teamwork to new heights. American employees were subjected to propaganda explaining how they were part of the team working with the 'men at the front'. Time and motion studies broke down every activity into its component parts, with the goal of making the human employee time efficient.

At this point of their history, the Americans proved to be adept at macro- as well as micro-planning. The introduction of the Marshall Plan after the Second World War was both shrewd and altruistic. It put Europe back together again more quickly than any European dared imagine in 1945. Without American aid (and protection) Western Europe's progress would have been slower and perhaps as bitter as that of the East's. That America needed a strong Western Europe to act as a buffer against Soviet interests is undeniable. None the less, those of us who grew up in the West shaped by President Truman, rather than the East shaped by First Secretary Stalin, have much to be thankful for.

After the Second World War the concept of the American team effort, consolidated and idealized as the 'Corporation', went a stage further. Graduates joined AT&T or IBM or Coca-Cola for life. 'You be good to us, IBM will be good to you.' The Corporation demanded loyalty of its employees like a mini-nation state, and like a mini-nation state great emphasis was put upon a uniform identity governing every aspect of the way in which the company presented itself and did things. The corporate identity affected the design of architecture, office furniture, office equipment and the graphics, publicity and advertising used by the company.

American design historian Esther McCoy has explained in her essay 'The Rationalist Period',[5] by which she means the 1950s, that exactness, standardization and rationally directed machines were regarded as an ethical necessity for the good of human kind. However, she does not say who regarded it as an 'ethical' necessity. It seems unlikely that workers would regard standardization of their jobs or lives as 'ethical'. And clearly not all workers did – they became militant, kept changing their jobs, going sick or going slow. As a result, the social science of worker management developed rapidly in response to an economically driven need to resolve the inherent conflict between enabling a worker to maintain his or her self-respect as an autonomous creative being and the requirements of production to simplify things atomistically (see also pp. 150–9).

It appears that in the USA the concept of 'loyalty to the company' was a part of an acceptable (if not necessarily universally accepted) belief that loyalty was a part and parcel of working for the common good. It was a concept that succeeded well in West Germany and exceptionally well (so it seems) in Japan. It was a fragile concept in Britain because employees were loyal to their class or their trade union or, less often, their political party. As a consequence, Britain did less well against the all-pull-together organization of the competition. Britain failed (no doubt for some good reasons) to adopt the most significant feature of modern industrial culture: the organizing ethic that had been honed – and was dominated by – the USA.

The science of management and the ideologies of corporations have not stood still. The more feudal elements of the large corporate structure are being dispensed with as corporations move towards a federal system, rather than a centralized one. Much research and debate is taking place into how companies can learn to live with uncertainty, how decisions are taken or should be taken and where and at what level the most effective decision-making takes place. We appear to be moving continuously and 'happily' to ever more consumer freedom and ever more civilized, democratic, interesting and friendly work environments. The worker–consumer is apparently well served all round by liberal capitalism. Who needs central planning? Hayek is a hero, after all.

But just as the science of management has evolved to the situation where the feudal model has given way to a democratic or federal model, the outside world has been evolving too. Alarmingly, the spiral of consumption also looks like a vortex. From being a spiral upwards towards material pleasures, we see a spiral downwards into pollution, waste and environmental crises.

Moreover, it is beginning to dawn upon a wider circle of managers and politicians that the spiral of consumption has so far only applied to about twenty of the world's several hundred countries. What will happen when, eventually, the USSR and China begin to satisfy the demands of their billion plus consumers? Liberal capitalism based upon the minimum of central planning and the maximum of competitive licence looks less comfortable when viewed globally. If the Chinese mimic Western excess, *they* are going to damage further *our* world.

So long as the third world remained simply poor, it was not likely to impinge upon the freedoms and values of the Western consumer. But the Brazilians and the Taiwanese, the Indians and the Chinese are showing signs of wanting to join the freedoms of consumerism. And just as we are waking up to the extraordinary damage we are doing to the environment through our lack of central planning, these others are beginning to unleash a quantum leap in environmental damage through their desire to enjoy some of our freedoms.

Ironically, there are now covert calls from the liberal capitalist West (upon the World Bank especially) for some central planning. And it is beginning to look as though, in order to create some greater good, liberal capitalism will have to be tempered with more rather than less central planning and that, to some extent, consumer choice will have to become restricted.

The post-Second World War culture in which design has thrived has been a culture based upon a mixture of co-operation (of the kind described by Hayek) and individualism – I want my car, my bit of road, my house, my freedom to travel in aircraft and so on. Good freedoms – freedoms which, if denied, add to the miserable aspect of life. Yet, to a degree, some of these freedoms may have to be curtailed – whether through tax or price mechanisms, rather than direct legislation, is not clear. Consider a very simple example. Currently 80 per cent of travel in the world involves the people of the twenty richer nations. What if the peoples of China, the USSR and India begin to get wealthy enough to travel? Consider the effect upon the environment of their own countries and upon others if a billion more people begin moving around.

So far the ethic of spiralling consumption has been unchallenged because the 'other' countries of the world are too poor to join in. Spiralling consumption has also been unchallenged because most consumers have not understood what they were buying. They do not know how their purchases are produced. Hardly their fault. The competitive element of liberal capitalism depends upon stressing the virtues rather than the negative aspects of a product. Advertising has ensured that the rupture between the 'below' and 'above the line' realities stays complete. Who wants to know of the violence of the abattoir as they bite into the burger?

Central planning (in the forms carried out under the banner of Marxist–Leninism) has not been a satisfactory alternative to liberal capitalism because the Eastern bloc countries have failed both the consumers and the environment. None the less, the late 1980s have seen an interesting change in the West – a willingness among the richer countries to consider some forms of pan-national central planning which will protect the environment even at the expense of manufacturing (and therefore designer) freedom. The European Community, with its centralized committees that are laying down standards on the environment, on safety and health, as well as civil rights, which member nations are obliged to follow, is one of the most interesting cultural developments of the 1980s, paving the way in the 1990s for the emergence of the EC as a single trading entity.

I do not, however, either 'advocate' or 'predict' that there will be wholesale centralization of planning. To advocate such a step in the light of the failure of East European and Soviet economic and social policies would be foolish. In any case, having begun with Hayek, it is salutary to persist with him and his warnings about central planning. He says: 'Planning on an international scale, even more than is true on a national scale, cannot be anything but a naked rule of force, an imposition by a small group on all the rest of that sort of standard and employment which the planners think suitable for the rest.'

Most of us in the free West will perhaps incline to agreement, but Hayek's commentary here is passionate and only partially objective (it was, after all, written during the Second World War). The EC, for example, imposes many standards upon its members to the benefit of individualism and individuals within the nation states which make it up. People who have been unjustly dealt with in British courts have gone on to find justice in the European Courts of Justice. 'The naked rule of force' is not an appropriate expression for the EC.

The EC is an interesting example of co-operation because its member states can and do violate EC agreements without fear of military sanction. The EC cannot impose itself through force; it has to have the co-operation of members. Thus, while the EC is not itself immune to shooting itself in the foot through being intolerant or even, on occasions, corrupt, its bureaucracies and politicians know it is in their own interests to seek to achieve fair and essentially liberal policies. The fact that member nations can walk out of the federation actually introduces an element of supply-and-demand competition into EC policies. Total political union would, probably, be a mistake. As ever, it is a balance of interests that is required – and federations and coalitions are a useful, albeit imperfect tool for balancing interests that need to co-exist.

Indeed, while one is right to fear central planning because of the power it gives to the few, it is a fact of life that it is always 'a few' who control, plan and exercise power. In a 'free' market economy, there is a *de facto* centralization rooted in the commercial interests of a few dominant companies in every one of the major industries. Thus, if it is true that, for example, the major oil companies compete with one another, it is also true that together they present a united front against anything they think will diminish their profits. Quite often their interests run counter to all manner of other desirable interests, especially environmental ones.

As always, of course, there is no blanket strategy which will give us the best of all possible worlds. But unfettered consumption on the *world* scale will defeat us simply because the size of the world's population, taken with the size of each individual's potential demands, will contradict one another. A tyranny of international bureaucracy would be horrible indeed, but in order to preserve choice and extend choice to the rest of the world, it *seems* that we have to devise a more mature form of consumerism and choice and generate a new, more subtle model of supply and demand.

Design, which now operates as an extended form of advertising or in response to a simple market demand problem, will also have to mature. The ethical and environmental aspects of where a thing is made, who makes it and under what conditions, what it is made of, how it will be used and how it will be disposed or recycled, will become as integral to the design attitude as style and fashion are now. Much of this necessary improvement in design (and manufacturing) sensibility is possible through the evolution of public opinion, itself fed by information, the provision of which requires, as Hayek would be the first to point out, a free society. No one system guarantees such freedom. Ironically, Great Britain, which has rediscovered the freedom of market forces, is now considered by some journalists in Europe to have a press which is only about fifty per cent free.

The post-War period has in some respects seen a history of *freedom through ephemera*. Perhaps the next evolution is *freedom through quality*, through conservatism, conservation and a greater emphasis upon communal interests. Design will thus come of age as a profession if it can help the world's consumers encourage these new, *communal* (as distinct from individual) aspirations.

## The American economy and 20th-century design

Since 1941 America has dominated the world economically and continues to do so in spite of the rise of Japan into a super-economic power. America, with its extensive armed forces, also continues to act as the world's policeman.

America has consumed more than any other nation this century. Paul Kennedy, historian and author of *The Rise and Fall of the Great Powers* (1988), measures the growth of the American economy in terms of energy consumed. The figures are of millions calculated in metric tons of coal or its equivalent. Thus, in 1890 the USA consumed 147 million tons and by 1938 it consumed 697 millions. No other country matched that consumption.

The importance of American economic strength for the Western Allies fighting the Axis powers in the Second World War was immense.

Paul Kennedy notes 'the most staggering change with the more than eightfold rise in American arms output between 1941 and 1943 . . . '. He also notes that American power in 1945 was artificially high because the rest of the world was either exhausted or underdeveloped. Like Britain before it, the USA naturally took the opportunity to consolidate its political and economic interests worldwide. As Kennedy puts it: 'Like the British after 1815, the Americans in their turn found their informal influence in various lands hardening into something more formal – and more entangling; like the British, too, they found "new frontiers of insecurity" whenever they wanted to draw the line. The "Pax Americana" had come of age.'[6]

Russia too was enabled by the war to extend its sphere of influence dramatically but, under Stalin, the USSR acted differently to the USA. Parts of Russia were devastated by the war and so Stalin did the opposite to President Truman in Western Europe: he stripped the Eastern bloc countries of raw materials, building materials and machinery.

However, it would be difficult to maintain that there has been a marked *Americanization* of Western styles. American style does not dominate design. There is a very definite American look, quite different from that of Germany, Italy, France or Britain, and we see the differences between the national styles develop strongly from the early 20th century. The basis of this American style is a love for the *organic*. And although its apotheosis is reached in Eero Saarinen's (1910–1961) 'tulip' chairs in the early 1950s, the fondness for rounded forms and a kind of fleshy gothic remains endemic in American interior, automobile and middle majority domestic ware design to this day. Organic fruitiness, the aesthetic of the all-American breast, is also dominant in much of the work produced under the heading of crafts in America. The cornucopia, the breast, and the organic form generally provide the visual metaphors of the American equation that material excess means freedom.

The organic, rounded sculptural form became part of the classical mid-20th century furniture design vocabulary through the work of Charles and Ray Eames. In 1940 the Museum of Modern Art, New York, organized a competition and exhibition entitled 'Organic Design In Home Furnishings'. It was won by two designers, Charles Eames and Eero Saarinen (who worked together at Cranbrook Academy of Art) in 1941. Influenced by Alvar Aalto, the Finnish architect who had

*Womb chair and footstool, designed by Eero Saarinen for Knoll International. Moulded plastic seat, steel frame, foam cushioning. USA, 1948.*

pioneered contemporary design in furniture using bent plywood, and who had received a retrospective exhibition in 1939 at MOMA, Saarinen and Eames began experimenting with bending on two planes (necessary if you are going to create a vessel effect from a flat sheet). Apparently Aalto did not approve of this sculptural effect; he thought the results were more akin to plastic moulding and that such treatment of pressing plywood into hollows 'violated the language of wood fibre'. The classic Eames chair is a broad, deep container, like a generous eggshell cut in half. It is furniture's answer to the womb.

The love affair with Scandinavian – especially Swedish – design, which America had in the 1920s, left its mark – for Scandinavian design takes its cue from the concept of the vessel and the womb. The protective, all-embracing form is the theme both of Scandinavian design and its social policies.

The 1920s, which saw a number of exhibitions tour the USA from Sweden, were a boom period. After the First World War America was financially invigorated. It had large stocks of gold, it was the world's largest manufacturer of objects and of food, and it had a large home market for mass production to be encouraged.

Paul Kennedy points out that *home* consumer demand could absorb all the increased productivity and, in 1929 for example, the USA produced 4.5 million motor vehicles (Germany produced 117,000). The severe succession of economic slumps during the 1930s in the USA took the other major economies of the world with it. None the less, the consumer demand of the 1920s and the continuance of some, not inconsiderable, demand in the 1930s, assisted the development of a professional industrial design constituency in America, linked strongly to the advertising and promotional demands of manufacturers of many kinds.

The rapid increase in demand, especially in the USA, for consumer wares such as radios, vacuum cleaners and refrigerators, gave a particular impetus to the professionalization of design as an acitvity in its own right. The impetus came from industry, which was beginning to perceive the marketing and commercial opportunities to be gained by adding value to their products with style and, furthermore, using the things produced to promote the company.

But we should bear in mind Paul Kennedy's statistics about energy consumption because energy, as well being the basis upon which production can proceed, it is also a commodity in its own right provided there are enough users to make the capital costs involved in generating it worthwhile. Adrian Forty, design historian, has a lot to say about this in his book *Objects of Desire* (1986), where he describes how soon it was that the owners of electricity generating stations perceived the need to create as many daytime domestic users of electricity as possible in order to even out the peaks and troughs being experienced by the supply industry. Generating equipment had to be sufficient to meet peak-time needs, but if these peaks were too few and too short in duration, it meant a lot of expensive generating equipment was lying idle. Hence the electricity industry was quickly encouraging the development (and the styling) of as many electrical machines as possible.

Styling in the electrical industry has a complicated, even contradictory history. But it was the manufacturers of electrical equipment who were among the first to understand the potential of a product that was able to advertise both itself and its manufacturer through its design.

One of the great successes of styling as advertising and one which gave a spur to the growth of the American industrial design profession was *streamlining*. This was the style of the period 1930–45 which historians in the USA have written up as 'the automobile age'. The car becomes a part of the house as the garage becomes integrated with the dwelling. The influence of car styles on other aspects of design becomes stronger as the period progresses. There is a form of Art Deco furniture that has since been tagged as *Streamlined Moderne* which is prominent in the 1930s. Streamlining was a general style in which every object, large or small – writing desk, radio, cigarette lighter, automobile and railway locomotive – was given very slippery form. Many commentators point out that most streamlining gave no improvement to the performance of an automobile or even a locomotive but as an expression of progress, the slick torpedo curving was *it*.

Moreover, domestic appliances such as vacuum cleaners, refrigerators and washing machines were taken up more quickly in the USA than in Europe. Therefore the kitchen became more and more 'machine like' and the concept of the planned, utilitarian modern kitchen took root in the American imagination well before it did in England or France or even Germany. This further encouraged pared down furnishings, and tubular metal furniture entered the home via the kitchen and the diner. The American industrial designer came into his own in the 1930s and he had less compunction about serving commerce than the quasi-industrial designers of the Bauhaus, who were too caught up in the 'medieval' atmosphere of a college which put ideas first and commerce second.

Even so, there was intellectual dissension in the USA. Philip Johnson (1906– ) curated a polemical exhibition called 'Machine Art' at the Museum of Modern Art in New York in 1934. In the exhibition catalogue Johnson distanced himself and the exhibition from 'style' and streamlining and argued for a more basic, therefore honest, vocabulary of the straight line and the circle. One of the interesting tensions in the machine age is that between designer as intellectual, wanting to serve the masses, and manufacturer and advertiser as providers of a consumerist cornucopia. The one saying: 'give them the plain truth.' The other: 'to hell with that, make it sexy.'

One of the first industrial designers in America was Norman Bel Geddes, who established an industrial design studio in 1926. He became especially famous for his overt streamlining of railway locomotives and, before that, for his radio designs for Philco. He, like other famous industrial designers who emerged in the thirties, such as Raymond Loewy and Walter Dorwin Teague, had a background in commercial art. Consequently, the idea of the object as embodying its own advertisement came easily. The influence of the American industrial designer also began to spread. Raymond Loewy, who repackaged a duplicating machine for Gestetner in 1929 and then went on to design automobiles and the Sears, Roebuck Company Coldspot refrigerator, opened a London office.

Since the Second World War, although advertising, consumerism and commerce swamped American designers (the 1980s fashion for post-modern and visual metaphors in product design has simply urged the philosophy of 'product as advert' along at increased speed), there has been a sustained, brave intellectual resistance.

The industrial designer Elliot Noyes sought to argue that use came before commerce as the ruling criterion in good design. It was *use* which made the new science of ergonomics so attractive for some American designers in the 1950s. And Henry Dreyfuss, who later became the first President of the Industrial Designers Society of America, argued the case for ergonomics in *Designing For People* (1955) and *The Measure of Man* (1959). A new version of this science is currently being explored under the heading of product semantics in universities in Pennsylvania and Ohio (see pp. 114–15, 175–6).

The lasting stylistic trends in post-War American design, apart from the abiding orthodoxy of the Corporation ethic, include a taste for the organic and also for literal and figurative design. There is a sense in which the gap between Europe and the USA is characterized by the greater tolerance or desire among European consumers for abstract design. Indeed, whenever European designers have sought to renew content in style – as in the case of the *Memphis* design studio in Milan (1979–1983) – there is a tendency to look to American style. Much that appeared as radical, post-modern, newly ornamented, neo-decorative in fashionable early 1980s European design could be traced to 1950s America or was to be found, alive and well, in the Italian–American quarter of Philadelphia.

The brightly hued and often exotically decorated plastic laminates and synthetic textiles of America's 1950s were ripe for ironic reference thirty years later. And, as has been said in the previous chapter, the liking for 'one-liner' content in design leads to the more intellectual but still very literal imagery of the new product design. Most design style is cued in from the demands of marketing and advertising; in the USA the connections just tend to be rawer and, sometimes, more obvious than in Europe.

## Design and consumption in Europe

The economic background to design and consumption in Europe is more complicated than that of the USA; the fact that the European states have twice gone to war across each other's soil can be seen as holding up technological and design developments. The recognized argument is that major wars are a spur to development, not a hindrance. But the case is not proven: trade competitiveness has proved just as conducive to development in the period of sustained peace, as competition to improve armaments was in the periods of intense war.

The establishment of the EC has resulted in a strong market, although as a trading federation – it does not yet match the power of either the USA or Japan. It could rival both, but for this to occur a greater degree of political unity would be required. As things now stand, the EC has much to fear from Japan although – as always in trade – this fear is not one-sided. The much-heralded debut in 1992 of one, single common market, with all (or most) trading barriers lifted, will strengthen the EC as a trading state. (There are those who fear an unholy trade war between three super blocs – North America versus the East versus the EC).

From around 1914 to 1935 the dominant design style in Europe's *avant garde* was confrontational, angular and edgy, but it was a style that was challenged throughout the 1920s and 1930s from various directions, including Art Deco from France and the passion for streamlining in the 1930s in America.

What we now call or instinctively think of as *modern* style, especially in furniture design and tableware, is thin, attenuated, spare, and frequently metal framed. It is fair to say that the modern style was given a considerable boost by the Bauhaus, opened under the direction of the architect Walter Gropius (1883–1969) in Weimar, Germany, in 1919. In 1925, it moved to Dessau, and industrial design as a separate area of study was developed.

The Bauhaus, however, was not the only nor, necessarily, the most significant institution influencing the style of European design. Consider industry, and consider especially a combine such as AEG (Allgemeine Elektricitäts-Gesellschaft, founded in 1883 in Germany). In 1907, Peter Behrens, artist turned designer, was appointed by AEG to provide visual coherence to a wide range of different looking products – electric irons, heaters, cookers, kettles, fans. The design or styling tradition that these objects possessed when he joined was based in hand crafts and hand assembly, and was, of course, pre-electricity. Behrens set about devising designs that gave expression to the technology that made these new products possible. The story of AEG is fascinating and is set out in *Industriekultur, Peter Behrens and the AEG* by Tilmann Buddensieg (1985). The particularly important lesson that AEG learned as the century progressed, however – as John Thackara has pointed out – is this: 'Confronted by growing competition and a diminishing technological lead, AEG came to realise that while it might make sense to the engineers to standardise covers, base plates and pointers, the impact upon sales of such a strategy was disastrous. A debate ensued . . . at the end of which the view prevailed that "even an electric motor must look like a birthday present."'[7] The results were both modern (celebrating the machine) and individualistic – the products possessed sufficient character to make them recognizably AEG and not some other manufacturer.

Of enormous influence, too, was the brief flowering of an *avant garde* in the USSR where – between the October Revolution and the succession of Stalin – there opened up a fissure of freedom in which the graphic and architectural arts exploded into influence. Modernism and abstractionism were nowhere more closely, more genuinely tied to political radicalism than in the work of Tatlin, El Lissitzky, Maleveich and a hundred others. Russia briefly but vitally gave modernism its passion.

In its abstract forms and logical arrangements, even a Constructivist-inspired wall poster acted as a metaphor. Its harsh typography and rectilinear forms, often angled and fragmented, conveyed a feeling of

*André and Paul Vera were French garden designers who married nature with modernism. In this drawing (1920), the fragmented geometry is reminiscent of Georges Braque's Cubism.*

energy, logic and change. Russian abstractionism opened the window upon the future: it gave a visual analogy of how the future might *feel* rather than what it would look like. The break with figuration and nature was logical: if the sense of the future was to be conjured up, it was pointless to do so with images of the present. The heroic idealism of the Russian artists and designers was, to a considerable extent, funnelled through the Bauhaus in the middle and late 1920s. When Stalin put an end to the artistic *avant garde*, modernism in the West rapidly became just another style. It went limp.

Chic modernism appeared more ornate, more luxurious than that which emanated from the Bauhaus. In the 1920s there was Art Deco – simple, elegant and with curved forms to the legs and arms. In the 1930s it became less classical and more brutal, with its hexagons, octagons, wedges and cylinders. It mixed wood and metal and glass with elaborate veneers and frequently looked like stage-set furnishing style. Fragmented light was another ingredient: in the hotel bars, dance halls, cinemas and bars light was bounced off hard lacquer surfaces, chromium metal, and bevelled edged, darkly lustred mirrors.

During the same period, from the early years of the 20th century through to the mid-1930s, Sweden was developing a philosophy of manufacture and design that put social awareness first. In Sweden, socially aware design rapidly became one of the means of expressing a commitment to building a more socially just society. In Finland, it is argued, design was seen as means of expressing nationhood. (Finland did not become independent until 1917.) Social Democracy links all four of the main countries. Social democratic governments appeared in Denmark (1929), Sweden (1932), Norway (1935) and Finland (1937). (A post-Second World War survey would bring Iceland, which became a republic in 1944, onto the stage.)

In Stockholm, in 1917 an exhibition of interiors had, as an underlying theme, social responsibility and this was writ large into the important functionalist exhibition of 1930 also held in Stockholm. This exhibition clarified an ethic in design that brought together traditional attitudes towards craftsmanship and materials with principles of clarity and modesty. The difference between North-West and truly North European design lay in the latter's more humane style.

As already noted, Scandinavian design made a great impact upon the American design community: there were touring exhibitions of Scandinavian design in the USA starting in the 1920s. The organic tendency in design, however, was aided also by ancillary technical developments; the gradual introduction of injection-moulded plastic forms is an example. For reasons connected with getting plastic forms out of their moulds, they had to be rounded.

Sylvia Katz explains in her book *Classic Plastics* (1984) that the first injection-moulding machine was patented in Germany, in 1926, but it was another ten years before the machine became capable of full automatic production. Plastics of various kinds were, however, popular throughout the 1930s and, explains Katz, 'homes in the 1930s were filled with brightly coloured, compression moulded eggcups and cruet sets, light fittings, cream makers and picnic sets'.

After the Second World War the rational approach to manufacturing and to design style – searching for an approach to styling that was 'scientific' rather than 'artistic' – found particular favour in West Germany. West German designers had learned quickly, along with some of the American theorists and practitioners, to take ergonomics very seriously.

Styling as science was given an impetus by the demands of the burgeoning military and civilian aircraft industry: the need (on safety grounds alone) to design cockpits such that the pilot, navigator and flight engineer knew what they were doing in increasingly sophisticated surroundings. Safety in motor vehicles also became a serious issue (although it first became a major public one in the USA when Ralph Nader published his criticisms of the American car industry in his book *Unsafe At Any Speed* in 1965) and helped to consolidate the use of ergonomics as the backbone of industrial design. Today, ergonomics with, increasingly, concerns about environmental impact are seen as the core of industrial design.

One of the more interesting of the design developments in Europe in the 1950s took place with the opening of the Hochschule für Gestaltung in Ulm, West Germany in 1955. This design school, envisaged as a successor to the Bauhaus, introduced mathematics, logic and sociology into its curriculum in 1957. It moved design further away from art and it begat a design style that used logic and rationality as its consistent metaphor. Its most notable exponent is the German designer Dieter Rams. Ulm and Rams are credited with the black box aesthetic so much mocked by the post-modernist youth of the 1980s. It was a beautiful aesthetic, but the intellectual justification for the style was made redundant by the very success of science and logic to which it was committed. With the development in the 1970s of the micro-chip and of the science of miniaturization, the need to give strict, pure forms to machines or electrical equipment was no longer justifiable by reason alone – black box design became merely one of a number of options that solid state, micro-chip technology made possible.

It is perhaps too easy to move from the pedigree of the pre-war Bauhaus, via the post-war Ulm school, to an over-general view in which all West German design is seen as orderly, rational and pared down. Certainly a lot of West German styling tends to express order and discipline and, indeed, in the 1980s some of the younger designers rebelled against the orthodoxy with subversive, anti-design. There was a sudden eruption of gallery exhibitions showing designs (especially in furniture) demonstrating against the West German middle-class orthodoxy. But the expression of order and reason has served West German

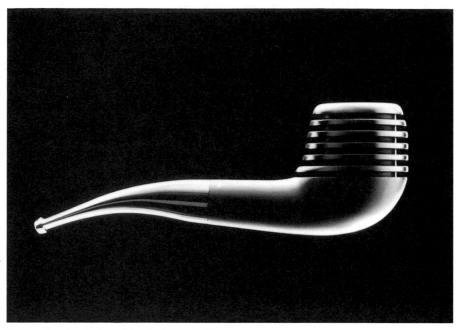

*Smoker's pipe designed by the Porsche design studio in Austria. Porsche design, backed by a very high standard of manufacture, joins the circle around puritanism and hedonism.*

manufacturers and exporters extremely well – encouraging and re-affirming the belief that consumers have in the quality and reliability and (excessive) performance of many West German products, especially motor cars.

The Italians realized earlier than most the innate silliness of searching for a single design aesthetic in a world in which technology offered such a variety of processes and solutions. Of the leading industrial nations in Europe, Italy was in 1945 the poorest but, with American financial help together with political support aimed largely at preventing an internal communist takeover of the country, the country began to expand economically. Italy was not and is not a country which has a great number of large companies, but there are exceptions like Fiat. In 1957 the creation of the European Economic Community, which Italy joined, helped the country expand further and there was an economic boom between 1957 and 1963 which gave great impetus to industrial designers.

*A post-modern celebration of one of the symbols of Italy's post-Second World War revival – the Fiat 500 automobile. Here transformed into a discothèque by Italian designer Vincenzo Iavicoli.*

Booms come and go. Italy has continued to succeed industrially, but in a fashion unlike other industrial countries: first, the continuance of many relatively small businesses has created a culture of manufacturing flexibility – it is still possible to describe Italy as a culture of workshops. Secondly, the regional competitiveness, the competitiveness between cities, still makes it possible to see Italy as a federation rather than a single state. This appears to fuel the idea of plurality, disputation, and questioning. Third, the black economy, work that generates wealth which by-passes the state (but not the people), contributes substantially to Italian success. These factors taken with a tradition in which, so it is claimed, 'Intellectuals in Italy have always enjoyed a higher reputation and greater influence than in English-speaking countries',[8] creates an ambience in which both designers and their clients are willing to experiment, innovate and speculate.

It is easy and wrong to caricature the Italian designer (who most probably will have trained as an architect) as something of a wild philosopher. Italian designers are given to the most immense pragmatism. Ettore Sottsass, one of the leading figures throughout the 1960s to the present, provides an example. In 1983 he turned a question about the desirability of planned obsolescence as a factor in the designer's life on its head.[9] Instead of giving the expected reply (planned obsolescence is a bad thing for enduring design) he said, 'Obsolescence for me is just the sugar of life.' But this was the moment when his famous loose confederation of designers under the 'studio' Memphis was just past its peak, having had an astonishing three or four year success in attracting praise for wild, ephemeral designs that set the benchmarks for decoration and novelty in post-modernist design for the 1980s. If anything was suitable for planned redundancy it was the Memphis style, with its funny 1950s American plastic-laminate vulgarity.

The post-Second World War symbols of Italian design include the Vespa scooter,[10] first produced in 1946 but sold in tens of thousands for the next twenty years, and the little Fiat 500 motor car produced in 1957 – both cheap vehicles for the populace. The Olivetti company began to advance its position with a series of good industrial designs in typewriters and calculating machines, and went on to keep this design lead in office and personal computers.

And Italy has kept doing it: the West still looks to Italy for a lead in what is good in design, and what is good in Italian design is probably the debate and argument, the ideological factionalism that underlies it.

Unlike Italy France supped with the Americans, but at the end of a long spoon. For although France made quite rapid progress after the Second World War in industrializing, she still retains something of an old-fashioned agrarian aspect to her economy. There is still a peasant class, still a large number of very small farmers – quite unlike, say, Britain. France sees herself as the cultural leader of Europe, but only just rivals West Germany in economic success. In the last three decades France has made a huge research and investment commitment in the fields of armaments, aerospace and nuclear power. It is, as ever, hard to gauge what the net bonus of a massively subsidized defence sector is for design innovation and technological advancement in the consumer industries. French consumer design is – very *French*. When one thinks of national characteristics as opposed to internationalism in design, one thinks of France. In so many ways French styling appears distinctive and sometimes quite brilliant – the Citroen DS 19 motor vehicle is an

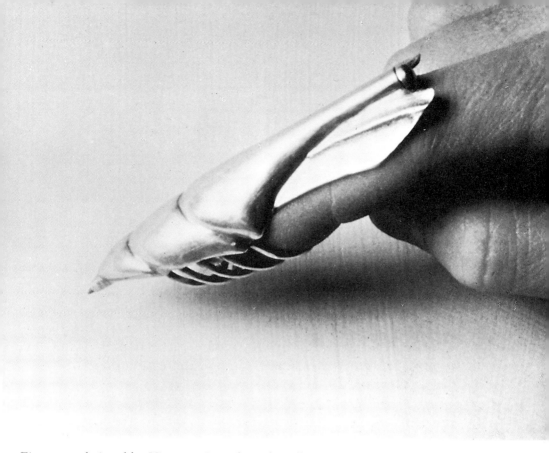

*Finger pen designed by Vincenzo Iavicoli. Italy still sets the pace in making design amusing.*

example, with its futuristic styling which expressed the technical virtuosity and innovation of the vehicle. Even in 1962, it had such advanced features as front-wheel drive.

Politically, as Paul Kennedy suggests, France has been extraordinarily adept in securing for itself an impact upon foreign affairs which is greater than its economic status would seem to merit. The USA may still have greater effect upon the world because of the size of the American economy, but its foreign policy pales almost into disinterestedness compared with that of France. This characteristic is worth noting because France also sees culture – its art, design and fashion – as being important in promoting France and helping to buttress the French language, French ideas, French interests against America, the English language and Anglo–American culture.

Prime Ministers and Presidents in France support and are active patrons of art and design. This creates an atmosphere of confidence. As in Italy, there is a shared interest in ideas – shared between artists, designers and industrialists. For one thing, highly talented, well-educated civil servants in France move with ease from government to industry to the arts to industry again.

The criticisms of the consumer society that broke in the late 1960s and continued across Western Europe and in the USA well throughout the 1970s coincided with recessions caused in part by the sudden price increases in oil as the supplying nations suddenly realized they could turn the tables on the West. In art, we see a sudden break with pop imagery and a succession of movements which explore anti-technology materials. It was the early 1970s which also saw a gradual awakening of the need for a holistic approach to design and manufacturing that would protect resources and the environment.

The Japanese strategy for breaking into European and North American markets came to fruition in the 1970s. British industry, in particular, lost out to the Japanese in motorcycles, motor cars, and radio and television manufacturing. Japanese design and quality of manufacture, together with low prices and reliability in performance, service and delivery dates sent old-fashioned and complacent Western companies to the wall. What was worse and what still baffles many Westerners, was a design and innovation into production system that enables Japanese manufacturers to bring out new items with astonishing speed.

Paul Kennedy points out[11] that what finally won the war for the Allied powers over the Axis partnership was the inability of the latter to keep pace with Allied production. Japan is now challenging every other economy through its speed in bringing technological innovation to the marketplace.

Against a competitor whose quality control, product range, delivery and after-sales service is so good, any advantage the West might have in design aesthetics is marginal as a competitive edge. Innovative, symbolic, metaphorical styling is essential in the battle for product differentiation – as a part of the advertising of the product. But such differentiation is only of use if the other elements of the equation are in place; as more than one automobile manufacturer has discovered in the

*National characteristics in design are often blurred. This silver cruet set was designed in 1987 by Martine Bedin, who is French; but the style could be read for influences from Germany, Sweden and Japan, though not the USA.*

1980s, a nice-looking vehicle will not sell if it is prone to rust or inept after-sales service.

Nevertheless, products are becoming the same 'below the line' and the advantage to the manufacturer lies in making the product stylistically different (but not too different). More to the point, much depends upon the style of the product communicating the right sort of values – the values shared by the consumer. Style is organized by reference to the class, profession, aspiration and age group of the target consumer group. What manufacturers demand now are huge amounts of information and one of the tasks under away in Japan – where manufacturers are fearful of the growing strength of the EC – is detailed research into national characteristics in design. Japanese design consultancies are now seeding themselves in Europe to find out which characteristics in styling matter most to consumers in each of the European countries.

It may be argued that what will emerge in the 1990s is more niche marketing, with styles thought through carefully (with an eye on their symbolic content) to appeal to ever more rigorously defined groups of consumers. Consumer groups, as defined by age, profession and the rest, will be targeted and seen to have more in common with one another across the world than with different groups in their own countries.

It is doubtful if national characteristics will disappear. It is quite likely that, in response to a period of internationalism in design, voices will be raised in favour of regionalism and nationalism. The most predictable design and cultural trend in the late 1990s will surely be a revival of conservative, nationalistic demands in Japan, a growing rejection there of Westernized and American ethics, and a growing awareness and demand for Japanese style for Japanese consumers. Similar nationalistic style trends may appear elsewhere, including within the EC – for here the bureaucratic hegemony of the 'Economic Community' may well seem suffocating by the late 1990s.

We must also hope for a pan-national recognition that consumption *qua* consumption may no longer be the primary characteristic of freedom. The ethic of spiralling consumption will be forced by natural forces, as well as economic ones, to compromise. Holistic design can play its role in a redefinition of freedom.

English design is sometimes subversive. Here Georgina Godley addresses us with a phallus whose design echoes the moon/phallus device used by Edvard Munch, a painter whose constant theme was sexual jealousy and neurosis.

# 3

# AS WATER IS IN WATER

# The Impact of New Materials

Three clear cultural changes are encouraged by the new technology of the late 20th century. There is a move away from a heavy to a lightweight and sometimes invisible infrastructure. And there is also a more perplexing change: the narrowing of the gap between what looks like nature and what looks manmade. A third trend, a move away from non-renewable resources, is also beginning to flourish in the form of research into re-usable materials, including a new generation of plastics in the automobile industry. These three trends will influence the nature of design as style and make sharper in the 1990s the arguments over how designers can help people feel comfortable with new technology without having to disguise the new with a packaging from the past. Moreover, materials science and information technology are delivering to us a culture in which our experiences become more complex, less substantial and, in the secular sense, more spiritual. Shakespeare has the right metaphor: modern times are becoming as 'water is in water'.

## The values of plastic

A plastic cooking pot contradicts the common understanding of what plastic is and how it performs: one fears that the pot will melt around the food. Ceramic or metal containers are acceptable to us through custom and because we know that metal is made in the foundry and that ceramic has been fused in the kiln. Thus both materials have come through the test of fire and are suitable for our cooking. But not plastic. And yet an all-plastic cooking pot is a possibility, if not yet a necessity.

The term 'plastic' is too general for a designer; it is unscientific because different plastics do remarkably different jobs – high-temperature plastics[1] are now being developed for the hot climate of automobile engines, while lesser plastics make serviceable shopping bags. But for the layperson the word 'plastic' conveys a set of values which may be out of date *scientifically*, but which continues to dog the designer and the manufacturer.

Over the years plastic has entered our lives as a surrogate material – it has been seen as 'standing in' for more traditional materials, especially metals. Plastic buckets replaced zinc buckets, plastic plumbing replaced copper pipes and brass fittings and, more recently, plastics have replaced metal as the main material in kettles and irons.

And during the 1980s plastic, in the form of the new (ish) carbon fibre and other composites, began replacing some of the important metal structures in aircraft and automobiles. And yet plastic is not a much-loved material and in spite of its ubiquity it remains anonymous – unlike stone or wood, paper or steel.

Consumers may not like or even notice plastic, but would probably, if pressed, concede the superiority over older alternative materials of the various polymers we use daily. A plastic bucket is superior to a zinc bucket because it is lighter, quieter to use and longer lasting. The modern domestic hairdryer is difficult to imagine in any material other than a plastic. Plastic has become the natural material for a number of

*The danMark 2 elite telephone, designed by Henning Andreasen (Denmark). It is difficult to imagine a more suitable material than plastic for a tool such as a telephone. Expressiveness in the material is unnecessary in objects that require clarity of purpose.*

objects: computer casings, pocket calculators, radios, clocks, food mixers, kitchen aids and secondary tools such as cling film, food bags and storage containers.

The molecular engineering involved in the variety of materials loosely labelled 'plastic' is extraordinary, but it is of less interest to the majority of intelligent laypeople than the visible engineering of, say, the carpenter. The cleverness in plastic technology is mainly 'below the line'. At its best the plastic artefact looks neatly engineered and as far away from handicraft as we can imagine. But even at its best the plastic form looks inert – it does not weather in an agreeable fashion and it feels neither warm nor cold. If you polish it then you make it clean, but you cannot increase the depth of its shine – polishing plastic is not like working away at the surface of some stones or woods. Plastic will not be burnished.

There are several aspects to our day-to-day intellectual and affective relationship with plastics. First, there is the distance that the process of producing plastic artefacts has from our understanding of how to make things. For example, you, personally, cannot do much to a plastic artefact. You cannot remould it, or carve its surface, or interfere with it. And whereas most of us have some conception, some knowledge available through the familiarity of wooden furniture or stone buildings, of what it might be like to carve stone or chisel wood or even mould clay and bake it, our lay imagination finds it hard to play with plastic.

Secondly, the very sound of plastic is dull: it does not resonate or ring out or ping – but thuds. Plastic things are mysterious in their perfection.

Thirdly, the tactile experience of plastic artefacts is generally unrewarding – plastic is smooth and lukewarm to the fingertips, not brilliant in its hardness like porcelain or steel. However, product designers are working – albeit rarely in an imaginative way – to improve the range of tactile experiences, usually by designing in indentations or ridges on those parts which are to be handled by the user. One of the commonest strategies adopted by designers seeking to enliven the plastic surface has been to pattern it – often copying natural materials such as wood or marble. The deception does not always work, but the intention is sound enough: we often feel texture through our eyes long before reaching out to touch (though most designers have yet to meet the challenge of tactile design).

None the less, plastic has been well suited to its role as a replacement material because it is possible to make it look sufficiently like the material it is replacing. Most plastic simulation is in fact rather poor, as if the manufacturer was making a gesture towards verisimilitude rather than a real effort, but at its dissembling best plastic can be most deceptive. There is a range of ceiling decorations of the kind that would once have been made in wood or cast in plaster but are, in fact, made in plastic. The simulation is so good that the chalkiness of the plaster has been replicated.

Plastic can be dressed in the appearances of other materials, but it cannot (with a few exceptions or without great expense) be given the 'real' qualities of texture, smell and sheen possessed by wood or paper. Plastic is so undistinguished that it provides a natural simile for shallowness and blandness: plastic food and plastic man.

But the plastic of advanced composites stimulates excitement in the popular press – if temporary and occasional – even in those people who are not scientists. Advanced composites are the dramatic *new* materials, light years away from the kitchen bucket.

A composite material is a combination of two or more materials bonded together to combine the properties of both materials, while, possibly, creating new or unique composite properties. Concrete is a composite.

Essentially the new composites consist of a polymer resin mixed with fibres of different types – such as fibreglass or carbon fibre. Each category of fibre has its own mechanical characteristics – thus carbon fibres are stiffest and glass fibres the most flexible. The fibres used can be short (about 0.5mm) or long (about 12mm) or continuous.

Composites get their individual characteristics from what happens internally for, as Ezio Manzini points out in *The Material of Invention* (1988), everything depends on the quality of the interfaces between the components and the characteristics of the matrix, such as a polymer resin. There are various processes for mixing fibres together – one of the most effective is the pultrusion technique, in which fibres are pulled through a chamber of resin to form lengths of composite of immense strength, depending upon the nature of the fibres used.

Composites like advanced reinforced plastics have been developed over the last three decades because European, American and Russian governments have engaged in an arms race in which military aircraft have had to become faster and more manoeuvrable, and have longer endurance. The demand was for 'low-density (lightweight), high strength and high stiffness'.[2] The military wanted stiff wings: wobbly wings restricted the speed of their aircraft. Professor J.E. Gordon, author of *The New Science of Strong Materials* (1976), provides a clear account of why new composites became an area of military need. The problem was that existing materials used in aircraft – aluminium, titanium, wood, steel and magnesium – competed more or less on roughly equal terms. An airframe in any or all of these materials came out at the same weight. The strength-to-weight ratio is critical in any aircraft, but the decision to go for faster or for bigger aircraft meant that new materials were essential.

Material advances in aero-engine design to make aeroplanes more powerful for their weight have been pressed forward by the weapons manufacturers. The armaments industry, so profligate overall, achieves impressive economic design in some of its particulars. The power-to-weight ratio of the engines in an F-15 aircraft is of the order of 8:1.

A high-performance carbon-reinforced composite is, weight for weight, about six times stronger than steel. The composites are very light (40 per cent lighter than aluminium); glass fibre reinforced polymers provide electrical insulation and other composites provide chemical resistance and freedom from magnetic currents.[3]

Commercial enterprise would not have developed these technologies in their current diversity, nor at such a speed. There had to be an economic imperative; and public money mobilized by political willingness to invest heavily in armaments provided it.

A new materials specialist, Dr Neil Waterman,[4] tells designers, engineers and industrialists two facts of life about new materials. Firstly, people do not set about inventing new materials in a vacuum, putting them on a shelf ready for someone else to come along and use if the fancy takes them. Materials are designed for specific needs, such as the aerospace industry. Secondly, new structural materials seldom, if ever, stimulate wholly new products. This is hardly surprising. Most of the things we design and build never work well enough: materials research tries to find ways of making existing machines more durable and safer.

Although a wonderful future for and with these materials has been predicted, in the early 1980s manufacturers were getting worried by some of the difficulties involved in engineering with them. A part of the resistance to new technology results from the fact that some kinds of existing industry are geared to a heavier practice, and quite different kinds of manufacturing procedures are standard – plastics are moulded, whereas aircraft and car bodies are riveted, welded and bolted together. Moreover, it can be argued that any production line is inflexible, in essence because production lines are set up to guarantee a set of results whose quality can be predicted – absolutely. Production is about the workmanship of certainty (see p. 144). Achieving this certainty is expensive: it takes time and money to establish production lines. They are not entities that accommodate change without expensive trouble.

Until recently there was still great concern over the impact resistance of carbon/epoxy materials. As far back as the early 1970s, the Rolls-Royce RB 211 engine ran into such difficulties with, for example, the engine's fan blades (they shattered if hit by flying objects, like birds). Rolls-Royce went bankrupt. (It was reborn and is once again one of the world's most successful builders of advanced aircraft engines.) Yet even now (1988) experts in other industries that have been expected to adopt new materials wholesale, such as the automobile manufacturers, voice doubts about the impact performance of new structures. In a detailed analysis dealing with plastics and cars[5] the problem is stated like this: 'Metal systems absorb impact energy by collapsing in a gradual and controlled fashion. A composite structure can also handle large energies by shattering, provided the impact is longitudinal, or head-on. But accidents occur from all directions – side impacts or vehicle "roll-over", during which there is a tendency for composites "simply to break in two."'

Consequently, there is a lot of research into steel-composite structures. In fact aluminium, the *traditional* competitor to steel, has also been developed in new ways to compete with the fancy carbon, boron and aramid composites. Alcan has developed an adhesively bonded aluminium structure that has been demonstrated on the Italian Bertone XI/9 sports car. Sports cars, being limited production, non–price-sensitive products, can adopt technology that the mass producers will not be able to utilize in a full-blooded way until the middle to late 1990s. A West German car, the Treser-1 roadster,[6] consists of an all glass-reinforced-plastic body on a hollow extruded aluminium frame.

Difficulties about impact strength will be overcome because weight will continue to be a factor in aircraft, cars, motor coaches and freight

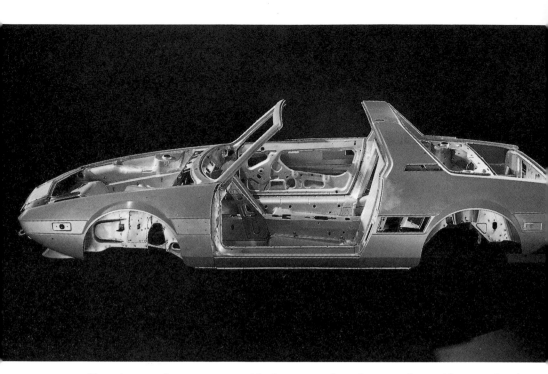

*Alcan has sought to compete with the new carbon, boron and aramid composites by developing adhesively bonded aluminium structures – demonstrated here in the Italian Bertone XI/9 sports car.*

trucks. Our passion for travelling light is forcing the pace of evolution from heavy and big to light and little or light and very powerful.

The 1990s appear to be set for a greatly increased use of advanced materials and construction techniques. One of the most interesting developments has already occurred in Europe, where an Airbus A310–300 has been given a carbon-fibre reinforced epoxy and aramid honeycomb tail fin. It is 20 per cent lighter than the metal tail fin and this leads to a fuel saving per aircraft of between 2 and 3,000 litres a year.

Composites are expensive. Science writer Thomas H. Maugh II, writing in the *Los Angeles Times*, explained that aluminium is \$2 to \$3 per pound, while the composites now used in aircraft are \$25 to \$40 a pound. Savings are made, however, by deskilling work and shedding labour. Maugh II writes: 'If a complex part has to be machined from aluminium then a lot of labour and waste is involved. Moreover, a complex aluminium part might be assembled from as many as 1,000 different pieces, including nuts, bolts, washers, rivets, and so forth.' But moulding with composites achieves a 75 per cent reduction in the parts.

If we look into the 1990s it is likely that aramid fibre, which is five times stronger than steel, but lighter, more supple and more fireproof, is going to have its day. There is *talk* of it doing to industry in the 1990s what nylon did in the 1950s. Aramid is a petrochemical-based fibre synthesized from chlorine and hydrogen to make a polymer that is dissolved in sulphuric acid and spun into tiny filaments 20 microns wide. The filaments are then woven into threads or moulded into pulp for plastic.[7]

## *The superconductivity revolution*

Advanced reinforced plastics are one category of new technological innovation; another major excitement in industry, which is set to have a major effect on the design of computers, is superconductivity. Its story starts in electronics, but then proceeds to photonics and it may end in biology.

Doing things with electricity means building devices that control the flow of electrons in a circuit. Resistors filter them, capacitors store them and switches divert them. If you want a fast machine you need fast switches. The early development of computers necessitated hundreds of valves and large amounts of conducting material like copper. The machines were big and heavy. As is now widely known, the liberation from weight and slowness came with the adaptation of silicon as a replacement material for wire.

Silicon normally acts as an insulator, but adding other materials to it allows more of the electrons to move freely. The addition of other ingredients is called 'doping' the silicon. Lines of doped silicon can be drawn onto slivers of undoped silicon. The lines of doped silicon form circuits – like wire circuits. And where differently doped bits of silicon are joined into a junction, it is possible to make a switch – a faster switch than a mechanical one.

This was the background to the development of transistors. These were then arranged in logical sequences on single pieces or slivers of silicon. Together with tiny pieces of other material to act as resistors and capacitors, they give you a neat little circuit board. Thereby the design of computers was advanced, for computers depend upon very complex chains of switches.

Something else changed also: no longer was design thinking in terms of single components, but in units, in sub-assemblies. The nature of a variety of goods – especially from the consumer's point of view – changed immediately. When a transistor radio or a stereo unit was taken for a repair, it was no longer the case that a single faulty part would be replaced but a section, a sub-assembly or even the whole radio. Consumers began to get used to the notion of: 'this is not worth repairing, it will be cheaper to buy a new radio/iron/vacuum cleaner.' The 'throwaway society' has some of its roots in 'below the line' design. Modular engineering, which is what underlies this notion, was the result of the 'systems' approach to manufacturing introduced in the 1950s.

Ever since components and sub-assemblies have just gone on getting smaller and more powerful and faster. 'Things', including electrons, go faster if there is little or no resistance. In 1911 it had been discovered that if certain metals were cooled to nearly absolute zero then they became nearly perfect conductors. The costs of the refrigeration and the apparatus needed for the cooling are all too great, but some scientists believe there will be room-temperature superconductors in the not so distant future.

The first useful device anywhere to be made out of new, 'high'-temperature (the term 'high' is relative) superconductors was un-wrapped in late 1988 – it was the fruit of a collaboration between Birmingham University, UK, and Imperial Chemical Industries (ICI), and consists of a microwave radio antenna which transforms all the energy put into it with 100 per cent efficiency.

The uses of superconductivity are in micro-electronics and computers; it is one of the keys to making computers operate faster. Even more 'glamorous' is its role in electro-magnetically levitated trains – those that float along their rails – and battery-powered cars. Superconductors will also have important uses in power stations, medical equipment and satellites. Superconductivity is a technological philosophers' stone.

But because speed is *the* quest, even electrons are too slow: attention is thus also directed towards photons, which carry light. Photons can be sent via lasers and it is assumed by some strategists that photonics will usurp electronics in various areas. 'Below the line' technology will be thus even further removed from the layperson's comprehension.

## The limitations of the flesh

The combination of science and technology has changed our conception of what material is – and what design and engineering can do. One of the more controversial extensions of science and design has been to move from 'dead' material to sentient beings. The biochemists have opened up another field of new materials design just as surely as the physicists and industrial chemists. Biochemists, for example, might well be dreaming of growing computers rather than assembling them.

The possibilities of genetic engineering could have a great impact upon the culture of design. Genetic engineering, if it reached the sophistication of computer engineering and software design, would change our relationship with the natural world in more areas, more quickly and even more profoundly than the computer and satellite have already done for our geographical relationships.

There is a common-sense, even commonplace distinction between building things and growing them. The relationship between human beings and 'the world' that is implied by terms such as 'building', 'engineering' and 'constructing' is different in kind from that implied by 'growing', 'nurturing' and 'cultivating'. Genetic *engineering* conflates the two categories; it merges two of the distinct themes in the development of Western culture.

In this case, the pace is being made by the economic imperatives of the farming industry, rather than the political drive of the armaments ministries. There is an 'above the line' and a 'below the line' in the 'design' of animals. We breed cats for their beauty; we breed farm animals not for their style, but for their quality as dead meat. Both are also bred for money. Theoretically, it should be possible to identify and then remove genes for things like legs and wings, thereby making it possible to 'design' livestock as more efficient food producers.

Some people are troubled by the cruelty of modern farming, but most consumers are ignorant because the majority of modern farming design is already 'below the line' – you see very little of the production process that turns a rather beautiful creature like a calf into a carcass. It is likely that with the use of genetic engineering the manufacturing of meat will become more, not less, hidden simply because to operate otherwise would be bad for sales. Current developments are highly questionable – they include a leaner, meatier pig engineered by the

United States Department of Agriculture, which is lame and very painfully arthritic. It is something of a composite material, this pig, being a transgenic creation involving both human and pig growth hormones.

## Pygmalion

As long ago as 1929 the scientist J.D. Bernal foresaw the possibility of a synthesis of physics and genetics when he published a book called *The World, The Flesh and The Devil*. Bernal predicted that eventually the body would be dispensed with, that the brains of people would be connected via machines, thus cheating death through community action.

Such a future seems bizarre and repugnant but, while we shrink as humans from interfering with ourselves, we have transformed so much else that the 'natural'/'unnatural' distinction is already blurred. This is especially true of the landscape which, in some countries, has been wrought entirely to suit our own convenience.

For example, in countries such as the Netherlands or England, the breakdown of the distinction between natural and artificial has been particularly striking. Developments since the 17th-century reclamation of land in the Netherlands and the 18th-century Enclosure Acts in England have made for an artificial landscape in both countries. In the 18th century, the English aristocracy altered the landscape to fit in with utopian views.

Even so, the Dutch and the English have been used to a clear distinction between artificial and natural imagery in their work – they have seen the difference between a man, a woman, a child and a machine. Although mechanical devices born of Newtonian physics and 19th-century metal foundries had parallels with nature – it is possible to see the human body in terms of levers and pistons – we have never felt confused about the discrete identity of man versus machine. Until now.

*The Material of Invention*, by Ezio Manzini, contains a tiny black and white photograph of a connecting rod.[8] It is made from composite material with orientated fibres. It is both strong and lightweight. It looks not like a 19th-century mechanical device, but like a human limb, stripped down to its muscles in the manner of a drawing by the 16th-century anatomist, Vesalius. The combination of our being able to make things light and very strong, but also to make them in our own image to the point where they are also almost intelligent, is a form of sorcery.

Of course, composite materials and muscle-bound connecting rods notwithstanding, there are other problems to do with distinguishing between men and machines. In the 18th and 19th centuries many men, women and children were worked as if they were machines – an important point because what is real and unreal, natural and unnatural, is to a degree determined by how we look at them. And, of course, how we look at things, what prejudices and assumptions we bring to bear, is a key issue for designers who are seeking to make bridges between a puzzling or threatening technology and the rich variety of idiosyncratic consumers.

Watch a computer-controlled robotic arm placing electronic components onto a circuit board, each component having over a hundred little pins which have to be dropped into a hundred little holes. The holes and the pins have to be aligned, and clearly it would be no good if the computer arm insists on crushing the component onto the board blindly. The arm is equipped with sensors to make it pause, adjust and try again – moving on if, after the third attempt, there is still a failure to match the pins with the holes. The design of the software containing the instructions to the robotic arm is doubtless the real triumph of the design; but what is emotionally arresting is the sight of the arm pausing and apparently deliberating. You are watching a machine to which you can attribute a frisson of human behaviour.

The animal/machine and machine/human being relationships in our material culture are revealing about our relationship between ourselves and what we create. The machine/human distinction has served our material ends formidably well, and that is one of the reasons why we have tended to downgrade all animals towards the status of machines: necessary so that they could become tools and not agents. And the development of machines has served our ends even better because, of course, machines have no feelings. You cannot abuse a machine except in purely material terms. But gradually the natural and hierarchical world of our material culture is changing. Categories are becoming elided – not yet to any profound cultural upheaval, but enough to throw up some confusions.

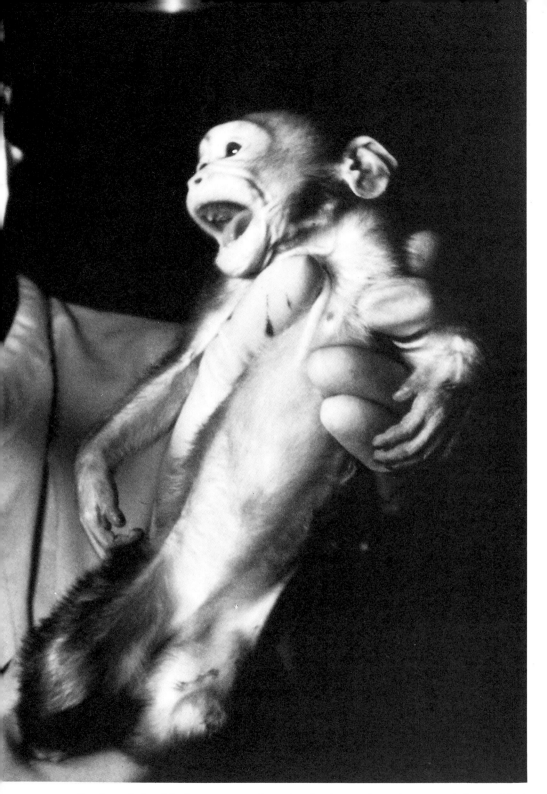

*In the relationship between people and animals, we have been saved from ethical niceties by the fact that most of the intermediaries between us and other animals are now extinct.*

Let me develop an analogy via the insights of Richard Dawkins, zoologist and author of *The Selfish Gene* (1976) and *The Blind Watchmaker* (1986).[9] He suggests that, as far as the relationship between people and animals is concerned, we have been saved from ethical niceties by the fact that most of the intermediaries between us and other animals are now extinct. He says that the last common ancestor of humans and chimpanzees died out 5 million years ago. Even so, we share 99 per cent of our genes with chimpanzees. Dawkins then reasons: 'If, in various forgotten islands around the world, survivors of all intermediaries back to the chimp/human common ancestor were discovered, who can doubt that our laws and our moral conventions would be profoundly affected . . .? Either the whole spectrum would have to be granted full human rights (Votes for Chimps) or there would have to be an elaborate apartheid-like system of discriminatory laws.'

The relationship, especially in Christian cultures, between human beings and nature, has been one of separation from the material world. It has helped considerably that the only other sentient beings – animals – have been far enough removed from us to enable 'us' to lump them in with the rest of the world. When we got lonely we invented God. We have had a very clear self-identity. Remember, Christians made God in the image of a man. This self-identity has been reinforced by the things we have made and designed. We make tools, design ornament and create a material civilization. But, even where we have created the most sublime sculptures of ourselves or other aspects of the world, there has never been any danger that we would be confused by what we had wrought. We were still clear on the distinction between 'natural' and manmade. Now, however, everything in the material world is falling within our design compass – we are beginning to redesign creatures and also to design computers that may lead to our designing intelligence. The intermediaries that Dawkins talks about are being supplied by ourselves. Indeed, it is possible that genetic engineers could make intelligent 'tools' of chimpanzees.

The development of usefully clever machines is dependent upon research in a hundred different areas. If machines are to become more flexible in the work space then they have to become more sociable too – they ought not to run people over or spoil other, expensive machines. Such skills are the minimum required of any machine that is to be allowed to wander around a three-dimensional space.

To give any machine (or any person) social skills then you need rules of behaviour; the machine/person must know these rules and be able to recognize which rules apply, and when. Knowing when to break rules is a sophisticated activity and somewhat too clever for contemporary machines. In order to be social you also need to have physical feelings – to know how not to bump into people, you need to detect them in your path. A host of sensors is available, but if machines and human beings are to touch with a degree of 'intelligence' on both sides, the machines must have 'arms' or 'hands' that have a degree of 'intelligently' motivated suppleness. In response to this need to make machines with a degree of sensory flexibility, there has been much progress made in the development of 'intelligent materials'.

And thus 'mechanical' actions come to look more like those of flesh and blood. For example, an alloy made from nickel and titanium remembers shapes. It will bend into a particular shape when a current is applied to it and return to its original shape when the current is turned off.[10] Very useful for 'finger joints'.

There are different sorts of mobility, of course. Myles Harris reports his discomfiture[11] when, having remarked to the Director of the Turing Institute that at least most of the most powerful computer systems are not that mobile, he was told: 'They are far more mobile. They can dial each other up on the telephone far quicker than you can move from one place to another.' Which caused Harris to reflect that the earth now has a new brain – its nerves are optic cables, its cells satellites and receiving dishes. Such musings might be dismissed as anthropomorphic whimsy were it not for the fact that computer specialists themselves discuss their specialism in anthropomorphic terms.

The degree to which academics in science or technology disciplines allow themselves to discuss technology in anthropomorphic terms varies according to the psychology of the circumstances in which the discussion takes place. In using animals in research, for example, the standard approach is to deny any human qualities to the animal – thus: 'it does not feel pain like we do', 'it cannot think like we do', 'it cannot have pleasure like we do'; and 'animals are incapable of emotions like ours'. This protects the human experimentor (or farmer, or consumer of animal-based or -tested products) from feeling bad because the subject has been turned into an object by means of ditching anthropomorphism in favour of 'mechanomorphism' (or whatever word we can construct to mean the opposite to anthropomorphism).

We are probably even more concerned to protect ourselves from attributing human feeling to machines. Yet, such is the distance we have come that the metaphors we need in our language to describe what is happening in modern technology are generated from the human body. And such is the blurring between manmade and natural, that we are now obliged to treat the earth's new 'brain' almost literally like another organism – one that can pick up infections. Take the design of computer software as an example. An extraordinary article published in the American journal *Science* had the following headline and sub-title: 'The Scourge of Computer Viruses – Software bugs deliberately designed to replicate in computer systems have the potential to wreak havoc; protection urged for military data. Is a vaccine feasible?'

The article is talking about the computer network as a body; it describes a computer 'virus' in terms of a real one. It states that a computer virus is a program that infects other programs by modifying them to include a version of itself. 'Like real viruses, these ones carry a genetic code, recorded in this case in machine language. The code tells a host system to insert the virus into its main logic system. Once established, the virus silently infects every other program it can reach.' The article soberly lists the nasty consequences of computer diseases, which include – ultimately – an attack by one nation's computers on another's. Some months after this article was published in early 1988, the concept of the computer virus had become a reality and it is now regarded as a major problem.

## The incorporeal infrastructure

Information networks, computer databases, systems generally, provide a new hidden infrastructure, the latest addition to a century of new systems beginning with underground sewers, railways, then electricity, radio, television and linked computers.

The move towards a light, almost incorporeal infrastructure is tied in with computerization as well as with the development of light materials. In fact the effect on Western culture of the moves towards the incorporeal is already considerable. At the relatively trivial level, we are seeing a change in attitude whereby *light* – as in lightweight or lightly structured – does not automatically imply shoddiness. This is a significant cultural change.

Western culture, especially European culture, grew powerful in nation after nation, century after century, through the accumulation of mass.[12] Mass and heaviness reached its apotheosis as both a physical fact of life and as a metaphor in the late 19th and early 20th centuries – the most potent materials were iron and steel. J.E. Gordon, in his *The New Science of Strong Materials*, gives a rapid insight into the metaphorical power of 'heavy' metal and 'heavy' industry when he reminds us that Joseph Dzhugashvili changed his name to Stalin, which means 'firm' or 'rigid' and is associated with iron. Stalin brutalized his people in order to make the USSR an empire of iron and steel manufacturing. His successor, Nikita Khrushchev, was really excited on his visit to the USA when he passed through New Jersey – the mess of smoke and manufacturing and iron and steel titillated his hunger for power.

Gordon suggests that people are happier working with wood than metal and that heavy-metal industries are traditionally unhappy places where power and politics combine. 'There is', says Gordon, 'a strong case that steel is the agent of a sort of faceless industrial oppression, the life-blood of the Dark Satanic Mills. Indeed steelworks are gloomy places.' Certainly the disappearance of the foundries in America and Europe causes no grief: what upsets people is the loss of jobs and the consequent waste of intelligence and skills – a separate matter.

The message of metal, the metaphor of metal, is not uniform – gold, silver and tin have different histories and qualities, while the intensely useful aluminium is, because of its lightness, less domineering than iron or steel. But, if we follow in Gordon's footsteps and reflect on the domestic landscape, it is interesting to note that while heavy wood is acceptable in furniture, heavy metal is not – except in the garden. And even light-metal construction has failed to have a big impact in the home except, perhaps, in the kitchen. The coldness and deadness of metal has made it less acceptable to popular domestic taste than wood.

Heaviness is associated with oppressiveness; the past is heavy and the future is light. But Heavy is also Secure. The reluctance of big institutions, such as banks or town halls, to give up their weighty buildings, their imposing façades and their grand entrances has much to do with the need to present confidence. Banks are now beginning to

*The art of engineering drawing reached its apotheosis in the mid-nineteenth century –*
*the poetic celebration of the machine was a modernist celebration of progress.*

In these three chairs we run through a range of both materials and construction. The high technology aluminium and polyurethane sofa by Jean Nouvel (below) and the advanced plastic chair manufactured by Kartell (opposite) are striving – by design – to overcome the unfriendly nature of their materials. The quasi-traditional Mexican chair (left) is, however, unsatisfactory because it wears the method of its construction and its anti-industrial aesthetic too fulsomely upon its sleeve.

shed some of their pomposity and some of their overt security, but this move is made possible only by the sophistication of electronic safes, video cameras and clever electronic alarms.

In a more general sense we are becoming accustomed to the science of the incorporeal in the same, pervasive way that we got used to the theories of evolution, or the much earlier Copernican revolution. Rumours of the tales told by physicists may have something to do with this, especially now that writers such as Saul Bellow, Ian McEwan, Tom Stoppard and John Updike[13] have begun making connections between us and the new science via their art. Certainties are becoming not so much destroyed, as diaphanous, harder to pin down. The landscape of small-particle physics has turned out to be a much more interesting *avant garde* than that provided earlier this century by, for example, the surrealists.

In Tom Stoppard's play, *Hapgood* (1988), we are told to think of the electron not in terms of those orderly, rational-looking billiard-ball models we had at school, but as being like a butterfly in the dome of St Paul's Cathedral. And in a peculiar kind of way, in a way analogous to that image, modern individual people are, courtesy of new technology, new materials, old art and their own mental and physical restlessness, like Stoppard's view of the electron. Flighty.

This new lightness of touch, this portability has given us tangible delights. A modern individual can travel 70 or 570 or (on Concorde) 1070 miles in an hour listening to Mozart and dreaming of pleasures. Or he or she can be walking in a street listening to Wagner or Rock music or the gooey trickling of an easi-list'ning tape. This is delivered to us via materials science; the gift of disposable, instant, portable music mediates between you and the world. The Sony Walkman allows you to ramble in the metaphysical architecture of music while maintaining some physical presence in a corporeal activity such as walking, driving a car – or handthrowing a pot on a wheel.

The portability and lightness of new technology is potentially quite subversive of both social order and democracy. For example, it is hard to see how a society that wishes to be modern and deal in the currency of modernity – which is information – could deny its citizens possession of micro-computers, modems, telephones in automobiles and telefaxes. But such tools are anathema to authoritarian countries because they are difficult to control. Like the printed word, the new technology subverts authority. On the other hand, we see new technology being used to control people – perhaps the most questionable development being electronic tagging of prisoners. The moral and political consequences of the light culture will become more intriguing as the century continues.

(Opposite) *This design from the Zeev Aram Collection, by Eva Jiricna, is reminiscent of the bottle rack aesthetic celebrated by Marcel Duchamp. (See also Chapter Four.)*

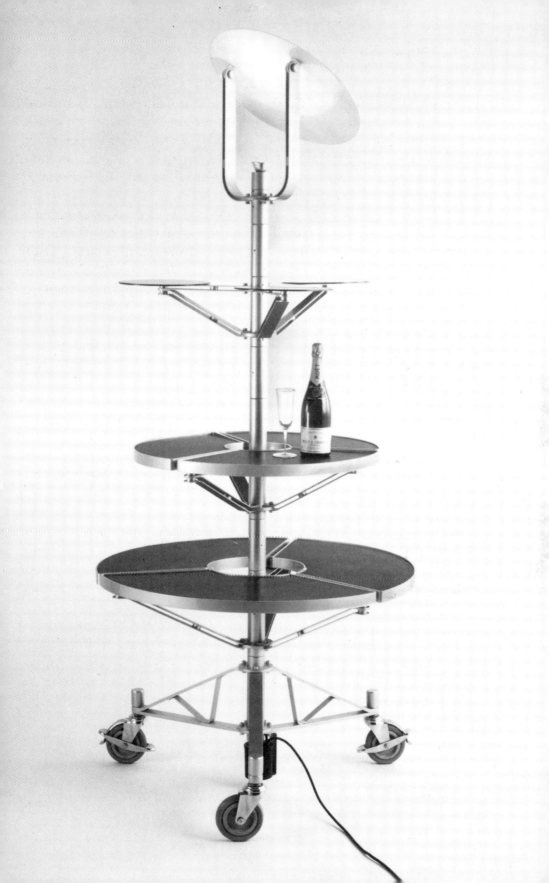

# 4

# OUR DOMESTIC LANDSCAPE

# Design and the Home

Seen from the viewpoint of the individual householder modern culture *ought* to look like an upside-down pyramid. The apparatus of the mega-industries pivots on our house. Yet it is probable that the majority of consumers have only a scant idea of the lengths to which our society has gone in order to provide improvements to our comfort. Some improvements – the provision of an adequate sewage system, for example – are obviously the result of thoughtful, farsighted people recognizing the need for common infrastructures for the common good. Other, smaller comforts, such as the development of the oven-bake French fry, are more perplexing.

What the consumer is largely unaware of is the diversity of industry required to make that oven-bake French fry. Holding one of the chips between one's fingers and looking back to where it came from provides an extraordinary perspective. Merely reviewing its progress from the factory to the supermarket reveals the following:

(1) the existence of an energy industry to support the manufacturer

(2) a petro-chemical industry to produce the refrigeration coolants

(3) a polymers industry to produce the packaging

(4) a set of graphic designers and advertising consultants to help to sell the finished product

And this is to ignore the pre-factory stage in which scientists worked hard to solve the problem of designing chips that can go from frozen state to hot oven without becoming uneatable. The potato itself, of course, will have been nurtured through a plant-breeding institute and protected from blight and other diseases by the efforts of an agri-chemical industry.

In one sense such a perspective[1] is a false one. The energy, chemical, oil, transport and retail industries were not started with the express intention of producing such a minor product. Rather, the existence and continuing development of such industries permits a constantly expanding variety of these little comforts. However, every such addition, while adding to the choice and freedom of the consumer, also adds to the overall problem of diminishing the earth's resources and increasing the risk of spoliation. Naturally, one need not pick upon the French fry. Outside the domestic arena, the defence industries are a more alarming, wasteful and incredible example.

That the 'ordinary' intelligent consumer does not connect the 'below the line' realities of manufacturing to the 'above the line' domestic comforts is not surprising. The gulf between your kitchen and the devil's is a gulf of values and meanings. The world of consumption has been marketed as friendly and creative; the harsher, competitive and, in some respects, destructive world of manufacturing has been disguised. It has not sat at table with you.

Nevertheless, those men and women who begat ovenbake French fries must have taken them very seriously – the French fries were designed, they were a technological achievement, their promotion and market share were a cause of worry or satisfaction, personal demotion or promotion. For a while they were the creative core of some people's lives; for many others, their production is their very livelihood. It is as well, perhaps, if we do not press too hard to find the point of any one particular product's existence; better to accept, for the time being, that production and consumption have no goal, they are themselves the apparent goal.

The most positive reason we can give to ourselves by way of explaining the apparent absurdities of our technological giantism and excess is also the most obvious: we are trying all the time to pull the world to our pleasure by removing, as far as we can, the possibilities by which the world can injure us. At the same time we are seeking, if not personal salvation, at least the oblivion of personal distraction by pursuing making and selling and yet more making – for its own sake. The exponential proliferation of trivialities is probably an unavoidable by-product of our need to occupy ourselves.

In this chapter the intention is to explore the relationship between the consumer and commonplace domestic objects. The second part of the chapter deals specifically with the late 1980s fashion for marketing design through the use of metaphors and similes.

## *Tools that extend her body and his*

We have an ingenious variety of tools in our homes with which we can cut, sew, heat, burn, carve and drill. The material world bends to our fingers in the kitchen or in the home workshop. Tools mediate between our imagination and the physical world; every new tool is a symbol of our capacity to imagine a transformation and then act on that imagining.

Remote-control devices are particular fun, they provide a power like Merlin's – the automatic doors slide open in advance of one's footstep irrespective of whether or not one raises one's arm as though dividing the waters. There is fun, too, as one punches away at the remote control, switching through the television channels, or 'squirts' a magic eye at the automobile to lock or unlock its doors. For a second or two there would be pleasure in pressing the ultimate buttons and watching, on TV screens, the world go bang.

The point of remote control is to save physical effort and time. Conceivably, then, there is some small significance in the fact that it is the television, the video recorder, the automobile and the garage door that have received the Merlin touch, whereas the electric cooker, the electric kettle, the dishwasher and the washing machine have yet to receive theirs. This minor lack might be explained simply on the grounds that since these machines need filling or loading anyway, the removal of the need to set a timer or depress a switch is such a minor bonus that it seems uneconomic to manufacture or buy. (In fact, companies such as Philips and Sharp are trying to integrate these functions into an 'intelligent' house.)

And so, unless we ever get to the point where it is understood that *any* woman's time is as valuable as *any* man's time, it is unlikely that the economically and ecologically wasteful remote-control devices will feature mightily in the kitchen.

The ingenuity spent in saving ourselves the effort of switching the TV manually is a decadent waste of resources, saved by the fact that remote controls benefit the elderly and the disabled (not that they are actually designed with arthritic or shaking hands in mind).

None the less, there is much to celebrate. It is easily forgotten how far industrial design has succeeded in making things work well and how far technological cultures have come in taking the pain out of physical and mental drudgery. Design's contribution to the removal of hard labour is one of the fundamentally virtuous characteristics of the design profession. It is this service, which is both practical and moral, that provides content and value to a designer's work. Or, to be more exact, the designer working hand-in-hand with the technologist. 'Below the line' engineering and applied science provide the ability, the designer provides the bridge with the lay user, ensuring, among other things, that the product can be used safely.

Design can only be assessed roundly by reference back to the cultural context. And currently the process of design, manufacturing and marketing is orientated around the sex of the potential purchaser. Gender-based design assumptions underline the domestic landscape; it is not only a question of which sex tends to use a particular category of tool that matters, but also which sex does the buying.

When it comes to buying tools for the home, women count more than men. Women still do the greatest part of the housework and nearly all of the work involved in raising children. Many, of course, also contribute at least a third, if not more, of the income.

Bodies used to be broken by housework. There is an eloquent, bitter and anonymous remark made in 1870: 'To a woman the home is life militant, to a man it is life in repose.'[2] Just how militant the home was can be gauged by the labour in domestic laundry work. Christina Hardyment, author of *From Mangle to Microwave* (1988),[3] cites the instructions provided by Mrs Beeton for a 'simple' white wash. Here is a summary:

Monday, soak sheets and body linen in luke-warm water and soda; Tuesday, up early, light fires, boil water. Rinse each article, rub it, wring it. Plunge articles into tub of warm water; go over each item with soap. Then put linen into second tub of hot water, rub and soap again where necessary, rinse and wring.

*Then* boil linen for an hour and a half in the copper with soda. Then rinse in clean hot water, then in cold, then wring dry, then hang to dry.

It is a nightmare, the more so because, as Hardyment says, 19th-century clothes were (a) more complicated than just these simple whites, thus the nightmare deepens as one moves into the more complicated garments; and (b) made wholly in natural materials, which are cussed things to keep in good order.

And then to the ironing.

The engineers and the designers who have developed washing machines, tumble driers and a variety of lightweight electric irons, together with the chemists, fabric technologists and clothing manufacturers who have developed artificial fibres, detergents and simple, durable clothing have eased the woman's lot considerably. And, more recently, the safety aspects of the equipment have greatly improved.

*We know the nineteenth-century kitchen offered wretched work, but there is a visual richness in the design and the style. Gutted of the pain that was once its penalty, it is fashionable with many people.*

But, not all women are joyful about their home life, nor are they clamorous after more gadgets or more expensive or user-friendly artefacts. Some, like Christina Hardyment, take the lateral view by arguing that laundry work, for example, should never have become designed into the fabric of our domestic lives in the first place: 'If laundries had become more efficient and cheaper', then the household would have been relieved of a great burden.

The ubiquity of labour-saving devices *is* a blessing compared to the dearth of them this time last century, but it is also arguable that the amount of time many women spend on housework has not declined very much. Why? Because the presence of carpet cleaners, vacuum cleaners, washing machines, and a treasure trove of cleaning, polishing and stain-removing chemicals has made housework a constant, daily task. Moreover, the barrage of advertising argues constantly for the need to clean everything for the safety and health of our children. Cleanliness has been expanded into a neurosis and as such it presents an ever-bigger market opportunity for entrepreneurs.

Adrian Forty, author of *The Objects of Desire* (1986), goes further; he thinks that the very styling of domestic appliances has sought to deceive women into spending more time than is necessary on housework by persuading them that the work is noble because the tools of the work are beautiful.

Industrial design has taken the 19th-century pain out of individual tasks, but the 'tyrannical assumption' (which neither designers nor manufacturers have seen it in their joint interests to question) is that the domestic work will still be done for free, in house, by individual women. No amount of styling, no amount of metaphorical re-designing of the individual domestic tools, alters this state of affairs.

Forty's scepticism is well aimed. There is a deceit in the marketing of labour-saving devices – deceit, design and marketing are bed partners. But one has only to re-read Mrs Beeton's description of washing day to know that the quality of housework for a lot of people has improved immeasurably. Of course, as Forty says, labour-saving machines are not as good as having servants but the demise of the servant class itself represents a colossal reduction in the generality of pain suffered through domestic tasks (see also pp. 150–3).

Hardyment's intriguing suggestion that housework should in general be contracted out may just shift the pain elsewhere: it is more than likely

*Stephanie Rowe's drawing suggests that there is a monstrous aspect to the routines of modern domestic life — less arduous than before, but narrowing just the same.*

that people doing this work will be poorly paid, an itinerant class of auxiliaries. The professionalization of domestic housework may not be as attractive a design solution as it appears; certainly not as attractive as the situation in which all women earn as much money as men, a condition which would thereby make it economic sense for men and women to share equally the work of their own homes.

Many women have careers, and they spend less time doing housework than those without careers or outside work. Of those who stay at home to be (for example) *mothers*, there are some who argue that motherhood is a vocation, an end in itself: the work that goes with it, including the servicing of the home, is regarded as important, fulfilling and also an end in itself. It is hardly likely that they are all manipulated into such a belief by the dominant male hegemony. Running the home can as easily be regarded as a creative or distracting activity as most others on offer to the majority of men and women. Everything depends upon the conditions under which the activity is carried out (see pp. 150–

*Ugliness can speak volumes. Here is a domestic tool with a 'heavy duty' message styled in a manner that seeks to appeal to both men and women users.*

3). Among the critical conditions are self-determination – did one choose, or did one have no alternative but to get involved?

Consumers can be cheated, however, irrespective of whether or not they want to do their own housework. On the whole, people seem to prefer to live in homes that are quite different in atmosphere to the factory or the office (even though, for the woman, it is still very much a place of work). The rugged, efficient functionality that characterizes factory or commercial equipment is not felt appropriate to the home.

The tools of her trade are made as feminine as possible even where this means compromising on the performance and the quality of the product. The industrial or commercial equivalent of almost any household tool, be it a toaster, vacuum cleaner or washing machine, will be more powerful (hence able to do the job more thoroughly and more quickly) and more durable. In an effort to make things lighter, more sprightly and more 'feminine', domestic tools are frequently rather flimsy.

Basic design, especially design into quieter motors and sound insulation, has been neglected. The noise of the domestic tool – vacuum cleaner and washing machine, and food grinder in particular – is frequently painful. These oversights show the limits of knowledge of male designers, who do much less housework than women and thus make their design decisions more on the appearance than the daily function; as a designer, you see where the knobs should go, but you do not necessarily set about using the machine for any length of time, hence noise and other aspects get neglected. There are other, not inconsiderable design flaws, concerning the maintenance and cleaning of household tools: they are often difficult (and expensive) to repair – there is no design for the home maintenance of home machinery – and gadgets such as mixers, meat grinders and fruit squeezers are surprisingly time-consuming to clean. (This is not just a matter of gender. 'Male' products, such as electric drills, are now equally difficult to put right at home by the 'amateur'.)

Designing by gender is, however, on the increase. It is markedly present in areas such as toiletries – beginning with the environmentally polluting practice of putting harmful dyes into lavatory paper to make it appeal more to the female purchaser.

A recent European example of gender design is the domestic battery charger. Modern homes use a lot of small batteries in radios, torches, and, especially, children's toys. Marketing directors refer to second-order goods like batteries as 'distress purchases'. The majority of batteries in North-West European countries are bought by women. Disposable batteries are not cheap but rechargeable batteries have not been as popular as one might have expected. The problem is thought to be in the design of the battery chargers – these machines are ugly: they look all right in the workshop or the garage but not the kitchen; therefore, say the market researchers, they do not appeal to women.

Designers have responded to 'the challenge' by feminizing the battery charger and have made it slimmer, prettier and more acceptable to live with, plugged into the kitchen with the coffee grinder or mixer.

Designers are benefiting from market research; and manufacturers, by manufacturing according to gender, appear to give the consumer at least some of what he or she wants.

In contrast, the tools that are marketed at men are more obviously rugged, militaristic and *active*-looking. Again the domestic equivalent is

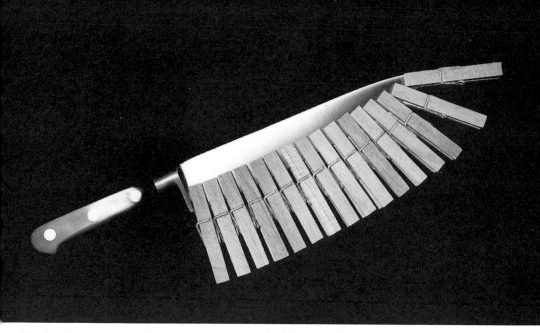

*The knife is an equivocal tool: it cuts at the meal table and in the abattoir. This tension is underlined here by coddling the blade with another domestic tool – the clothes peg or pin.*

seldom as good as the industrial one because, say manufacturers, the domestic tool gets less use than the industrial one.

That some tools look aggressive is not, of course, simply a result of macho styling. Function dictates form more often than not. You cannot have an entirely non-aggressive-looking circular saw, chain saw or electric drill. Nor for that matter can a scythe or an axe or a hammer look entirely safe. Even a bread knife carries with it an implicit threat.

There is an excitement about these kinds of tools that derives from the clarity with which they declaim their function. There is also something virtuous in their purpose – they are born with a role and the role is to fulfil a real need. If you are able bodied, you do not need a remote control for the television, but you need these tools to alter the world. You may not *need* ovenbake French fries, but to interfere with the world you need tools to cut, slice, rip, grind and drill. Small wonder that designers enjoy designing these things – to design a tool is to share in the virtue of necessity and the protestant values of helping another person do a proper job.

Tools are also communal in their imagery – the functions, which they cannot help expressing, carry with them a culture of making and a culture of power: the power to transform. Thus, with a hammer, we recognize that it drives in nails, that it is one of the fundamental tools of (Western) civilization. A hammer is a virtual necessity for making a durable shelter. The hammer carries with it the associations of transforming a part of the world. The simplest tool thus magnifies one person's power. Some artefacts, such as bowls, are – by comparison – pacific objects. They are for the quiet times, for rest, for contemplation and similar purposes.

Tools, however, are assertive. And how. Consider, for the purpose of illustration, the archaic scythe. Elaine Scarry, philosopher, discusses tools in her book *The Body in Pain* (1985). The cut made by a scythe, she writes, is a much greater change than anything possible by the arm alone – this is an alteration, not only of scale, but of duration. The cut grain is the free-standing record of a person's single action – it endures long after the person has left the site. Even lighting a match leaves the charred matchstick as a mark of the 'event'.

Tools are also things of attack. Consequently, one does not have to look far to find a Janus-faced pair of metaphors lurking in the design of many tools. This, too, is well explained by Elaine Scarry, who points out that the majority of tools are also weapons: 'The hammer that hammers a man to a cross is a weapon and the hammer used to construct the cross itself is a tool.'[4]

Almost any tool can become a weapon; Scarry says that as soon as the hammer or the knife touch sentient flesh, then the tool becomes a weapon. When it touches non-sentient flesh, it becomes a tool again: you carve a piece of wood, you wound a person or an animal.

The morally confusing mixing of metaphors that occurs wherever tools are styled up as weapons is more than pandering to machismo excitement, it is subversive of the social and moral good order that distinguishes between creation and mutilation.

Naturally, however, wherever designers seek to introduce reassurance, comfort, domesticity, the expression of power is quickly dampened down and removed. Thus the executive car is lounge-like in its seating and even in the inside of those most masculine objects, the long-distance trucks, the message is subdued.

These days you could argue that the feather-light steering, finger-tip controls, armchair seating, built-in bedroom and air conditioning have made the cab more domestic, more pacific, more feminine. The notion of describing it as either feminine or masculine then becomes irrelevant; what it amounts to is a pleasanter, more efficient working environment.

## The soul of the machine

The modern world has generated many pseudo-tools, objects which look like tools, function as tools when used by professionals but which are purchased more often by amateurs who buy them for their own sake. The massive growth in leisure and hobbies has fuelled this phenomenon.

In some examples it is doubtful if one can say which matters most — the hobby or the things required to pursue the hobby. In amateur photography, for example, there is a vast array of cameras and accessories to be collected. It is the ideal hobby for anyone who develops a fetish for engineered knick-knacks; many individuals may be amateur photographers *only* because of the equipment. In photography, as with other leisure pursuits (fishing, gardening, shooting, sailing) the hobby provides the excuse for buying the stuff; the stuff, in turn, is given coherence by the hobby. The pleasure is in the potentially fetishistic emotions that the equipment generates in the user. A fetish is the worship of an inanimate object to the point of excessive reverence or adoration. It is sometimes equated with irrationality, obsession and, of course, sex. And little imagination is needed in order to realize that playing with camera equipment and taking photographs has sexual connotations.

A part of the fetish is the excess of quality built into the camera, a quality and performance that exceeds need — such as shutter speeds measured in terms of 1/4000th and 1/8000th of a second. Much of the quality is not just excessive; it is unusable because the owner does not know how to use it or what to do with it.

The range of equipment available to the photographer is immense. The hobbyist is never at a loss for something to buy, something more to want, something more to save up for: power winders; speed finders; nicad chargers; film chambers; angle finders; auto bellows; duplicators; remote switches; lenses of various sizes, both wide and wider angled; close-up and telescopic lenses; filters, including soft focus, colour and polarizers; flash systems; tripods; and special containers to put it all in.

Everything has its name and number and, extending the comments above on gender-directed design, we can observe that photographic equipment is militaristic in its nomenclature: Nikon N4004 Decision Master; Canon F-1 AE Finder; Minolta X-700; Canon EOS 650; they could be variable geometry swing-wing fighter bombers or multiple-warheaded ICBMs. If they said Chuck Yeager flies a Canon F-1 AE Finder, you'd have to believe them.

But consider even the aesthetic pleasures of handling a camera of the common, single-lens reflex 35mm variety.

First of all, it is possible that for men there is a parallel between fiddling with a camera – changing the lenses, loading and unloading film, for example – and the loading of a gun. And the gun has phallic associations. After all, there have been enough films on the cinema and television screen that linger in image and sound over the assembly of a gun and the preparation for a shoot.

With both guns and cameras there is a triple pleasure of touching finely engineered metal, or, more often these days, high-quality plastic components, feeling the weight of these components in the hand, and hearing the sounds of components sliding neatly over one another or being swivelled, ratcheted or locked into place.

This is what it is like changing a lens on a 35 mm camera: you feel the weight of the lens as you unlock it and unscrew it from the camera body. You are aware of the precious weight of the two main parts, which must be treated with care – to drop either would be to dent the flawless engineering (and these things are expensive). The cleanliness of the parts is attractive. And then there is the deliciously rich sound as the new lens is fitted and locked into the body; it is a mellow, hollow sound, like the cupping of coconut shells, one on top of another. The locking of the lens into the body is satisfyingly precise.

In using the camera manually there are more sounds to enjoy – if you are a serious amateur or hobbyist (the casual user, the majority of us, uses a clever, but idiot-proof machine that is automatic and does not encourage the more sensory pleasures of taking pictures.) There is the precise ratchet feeling in the fingers as the F stop is positioned, quite different to the soundless, smooth, oil-on-oil movement of the lens as it is focussed. Winding on the film, one's finger moves back the lever in a long satisfying mechanical pull and, when the shutter button is depressed, there is the magical almost infinitely quick slice of the shutters snapped open and shut. The pressing of the shutter is deliberate, irreversible. It is as final as the pulling of a trigger.

For centuries one of the major ambitions of European cultures has been the achievement of flawless manufacturing and mechanical precision (which the ingenuity of the USA eventually satisfied on its own until first Germany and, latterly, Japan, caught up). This century has been triumphant in its pursuit of precision – of making things with ever finer tolerances. (Science, of course, has become almost voluptuous in its preciseness: chemists working on exploring photosynthesis in plants measure bursts of light in millionths of a single second.) Lenses and measuring devices, for navigation, for science and for engineering had to become ever more refined because on their refinement – and their reliability – depended the success of a journey, an experiment, a construction.

The aesthetic pleasure, the sensory pleasure that finely made tools offer us is almost a by-product of their function; but it is a by-product of enormous potency because of its relationship to a set of basic values that are bound up with truth, absolutes and constancy. The beauty of an accurate camera is in no small degree bound in with the fact that its mechanical operations are truthful (the reality its photographs portray is another matter altogether). The engineered tolerances are not in a symbolic relationship with the function of the tool, they are the function. The disciplined workmanship of the engineering is not *simply* an expression of integrity, it is the guarantor of the integrity.

Fine tolerances are evidence of good workmanship, good workman-ship constitutes a moral relationship between one person and another – it is an act of dependable, positive, optimistic service. Bad workmanship is cynical, subversive, nihilistic. The soul of the machine is the integrity of the designer and the designer's engineer and the designer's craftsman.

The irony is, as has been mentioned, that with cameras, the photographs are often unimportant. Or, if important, they are so not because of their aesthetic or documentary merit but as a way of testing the efficacy of the machine, testing its integrity, testing its soul. Apart from this the photographs are often worthless or, at any rate, quickly unregarded.

One of the reasons for labouring the sensory aspects of a modern, machine-made artefact is to correct the assumption that modern products are lacking in expressiveness. It is not true that an industrially produced object is *necessarily* less satisfying to all the senses than a handcrafted one.

It is true, however, that far from all industrial products have anything like the emotive, sensory appeal of the kind of camera described above. The unsatisfactory nature of their being is not necessarily an imperfection in the overall performance, or their finish, and hardly at all in their decoration or the cleverness of their expressiveness. For example, in recent years the injection-moulded plastic 'jug' electric kettle has become popular; it can safely boil a small or a large amount of water and, because the handle is on the side opposite the spout, like a jug, you do not burn your fingers on the last sighs of scalding steam, as you do with the conventional kettle.

As an expressive object the plastic jug kettle is interesting enough. In its general appearance it looks like a surgical boot: it is rounded, padded, puffy, similar to the sort of rounded tool astronauts carry into space (where roundedness is a practical necessity since sharp edges are doubly dangerous in the space environment). The jug kettle expresses safety.

But as an object to handle, these kettles are let down by the awkward fitting of the lid and, in some cases, the sponginess of the switches. There is no precision in the feel of the parts. These are small matters, but it is in these that the attractiveness or non-attractiveness of an object can rest. One struggles to get the lid off, it often slips into the jug, one feels that bloodymindedness is built into the design.

However, more and more we find we can take the quality of production and even the sensible design of an object for granted. And as we do so, we find that designers and manufacturers search out new ways to make their products not merely attractive, but fanciful. In engaging our interest, 'they' (those who seek our money) are being persuaded by designer stylists that 'they' must catch at our emotions.


*Emoting about the object*

The 1980s generation of graduate product designers has grown up in the post-modern aesthetic, taking part in but not initiating the rebellion against the modernist belief in classical, ideal form. How does such a young designer think? Alexander Groenewege, from the Netherlands, was asked by the design manager (for small domestic appliances) to make some suggestions for a range of hairdryers that Philips would produce in the 1990s. These products had to compete with Japanese products (everywhere in the industrialized world Japan sets the competition).

The general qualities that Groenewege had to aim for were obvious but, in some degree, contradictory: *solid* quality, but with *fun* and *personality*. The design had to be appropriate to the status of the purchaser, reflect something of that person's lifestyle. The detailing was to be *perfect*, the design innovative.

Interestingly enough, in the context of the earlier discussion about 'tools', Groenewege remarks: 'therefore, what one wants is something *nice* for the hand and the eye – and, because this is a product which you bring close to your face, then rational thinking rejects a design which looks like a gun.'

Groenewege mused on a variety of images; he claims that with the hairdryer he has devised, he wants to put fantasy into high gear: 'Drying your hair you start dreaming about waving palm leaves along Pacific beaches, Spanish Flamenco dancers, Japanese geishas . . . everyone has his [sic] own thoughts.' Moreover, he wanted the design to have a silent beauty even when it was switched off and left on the bathroom or dressing-room table.

In reviewing how he developed the image of the hand-held, non-technological fan as the basis for his hairdryer, Groenewege retraced his steps as follows:

*imagery*

- I did not begin with 'form follows function'.
- I started with wind, not with the thing that produces it.
- Then I thought about things that pushed and pulled and floated in the wind – feathers, birds, aeroplanes, wings, palm trees, leaves.
- Put *style* and wind together and you have a peacock.
- A peacock's fan tail is like a fan that Spanish women use to wave air. But a fan is also a communication tool and it depends how the women handle the fan, how they hold it the hand, how close it is to the face, how it is placed on a table. Is it dropped, meaningfully, to the floor, or snapped shut loudly?

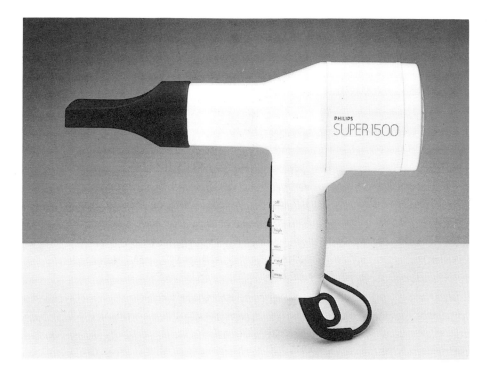

- The fan has a lot of hidden temper to it: rhythm, flamenco, tension, tenderness.
- In my imagination then the step to Japan (a styling and competitive must for my product) was not so big.

*technology*

- I needed body volume to contain the motor.
- It is usual for the motor chassis and external case to be one unit; I wanted them separated. This allows new styles to be built around the one unit. A step towards flexible production. The same unit can be fitted in a variety of different forms attracting different groups of consumers. Niche marketing.
- I also developed the dryer to hang on a cord because the Japanese like to use driers with their hands free.

Apart from being a good designer, Groenewege is disarmingly honest. Although he has (surely correctly?) rationalized his rejection of the 'gun'

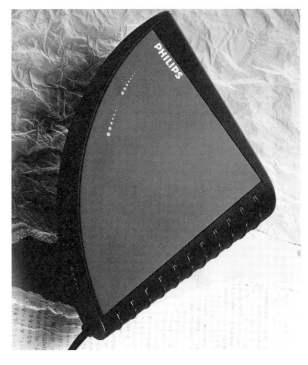

The simile of the gun is present in a surprising number of domestic tools – but then the gun is a naturally *useful* form. However, such imagery was rejected by Alexander Groenewege in this 'Fan' hairdryer designed for Philips. He wanted to elicit the allusion to hand-held fans, to grace, flight and air.

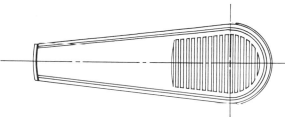

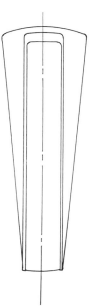

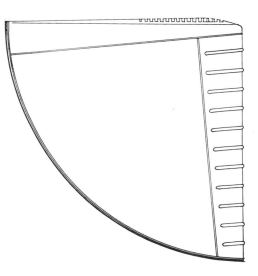

shape for his hairdryer, he also acknowledges the driving force of product differentiation. He does not want his product to look like existing versions (nor does his client). He says that existing designs, such as those by Braun or Atlantic Design, are very good but that they are 'too well known, too much copied to surprise me'. Novelty, not necessity, is the engine of product development, especially in products that are mature – where they have been around for years, and where fighting for an increased market share of as little as 3 per cent can mean a considerable difference to company profits.

Very few designers, or their clients, like to leave a product unimproved; they are forever seeking 'faults' in existing products that they can 'correct' and thus use as a justification for the new development. In mature products these faults are seldom purely imaginary, but nor are they fundamental. In this instance Philips had requested in their brief that the hairdryer's nozzle should be fully variable and fully integrated; the company did not want a design that used additional, clip on nozzles (which people tend to lose).

Not all products of our time are as susceptible to designer improvement as, say, electrical or electronic goods which, by their very nature, have a more decisive and divisive split between 'below' and 'above the line' design considerations. The bicycle, for example, a perfect example of the tool that extends the human body, is very difficult to improve – although people keep trying. Graham Vickers, a design journalist and bicycle buff, comments: 'Basically unchanged for half a century, the familiar "safety" bicycle poses a unique design challenge in a society accustomed to the regular reshaping of its most cherished objects.' The bicycle is intolerant of designers' whims because, says Vickers, any infelicity in the design immediately causes pain to the rider. There have been successful re-designs but only after re-designing the brief, such as demanding a lightweight bicycle that can be folded away for easy transportation. (The design, building and craftsmanship of the best bicycle frames are discussed in the next chapter.)

The bicycle frame is an appropriate modernist object and it is quite refreshing that it stubbornly resists re-working. But what is it that the late 20th-century designer opposes in modernism? The immediate answer is that the post-modern designer opposes anonymity and mystery, he and she oppose objecthood and praises clear subject matter, story telling and openness. The object is replaced with the word.

*Hairdryer for men by Atlantic Design (UK). It is clearly masculine in its bulk and machined imagery, taking its finesse from the styles of the 1930s.*

But the immediate answer is only partial. There are other reasons why, at this stage of the century, there is a pressing demand for objects and buildings to express meaning. Intellectually the demand for designers to think about the expression of meaning and the generation of metaphor in the work has some roots in the scepticism which underlies the wider post-modernist debate. Individuals, including designers, need to have frameworks and justifications for what *they* are doing: post-modernist theory has pulled the rug out from under some of the older certainties.

The most fashionable post-modernist theorist of the 1980s, at least among the English, Dutch and Americans, has been Jean Baudrillard, the French sociologist. He has apparently shown that there is no such thing as objective 'truth' or 'falsity'. Philosophers have done this before, and those from other disciplines have reached analogous conclusions. Indeed, in the landscape of the new physics it appears that subjective judgments affect supposedly objective events. It appears that in small particle physics there is a case for saying that truth lies in the eyes and mind of the beholder.[5]

Baudrillard has concentrated his observations on some of the phenomena characterizing contemporary consumerist cultures: namely the impact and integration into our lives of television, computer and video technology with the information that these media convey. Taken together, the technology and the information have added to the 'them and us' situation whereby 'they' seek to influence us by (a) finding out what we are like in order to (b) sell us that which we would buy because we like it. It is an arrangement that applies to the manufacture and consumption of anything – products, politics, ideas and even information itself.

The view that Baudrillard develops is attractively nightmarish because it appears to make flesh the kind of science fiction or Brave New World utopia with a sting in it with which we like to terrify and tease ourselves. He has presented us with a view of our culture that shows it to be a hall of mirrors. The subject matter, the images and reflections, are made from information about ourselves – our hopes, fears, ambitions, loves and desires. These are, apparently, re-configured into fantasy-facts as products, as advertising and as 'news'. A ping-pong game has ensued: we half-believe the picture of ourselves. Those half-beliefs become part of us. This 'us' is in turn reflected and re-presented once more by the hall of mirrors. We absorb some more. 'Reality' disappears, and with it truth and falsity. Or, in Baudrillard's own (translated) words, 'we will never in future be able to separate reality from its statistical, simulative projection in the media' (*Simulacra and Simulations*, 1981).

The irony, given that truth is chimerical on Baudrillard's reading, is that there is some truth in Baudrillard's argument.

The whole success of selling things depends upon selling people what they like and what they want, or what they can be persuaded to like and to want. Moreover, this entails not merely the heightening of the reality of whatever makes an object or a politician desirable to us, but also a dampening down of any reality that is deeply unpleasant.

However, Baudrillard has over-dramatized the completeness of the illusory nature of contemporary, televisually organized reality. It is not true that we are unable to distinguish lies from truths. We are forced to recognize the complexity of events and the complexity of contemporary culture; but one of the aspects of late 20th-century culture that Baudrillard ignores is the extent of the probing by a great variety of pressure groups and lobbyists of all those who seek to mislead, trick or cajole us into seamless, unquestioning consumption. The televisual reality of contemporary Western or Westernized culture is only one aspect of that culture. Many people have the wit and the apparatus not to stay in Baudrillard's hall of mirrors, but to wander outside and search for the people fixing the structure. Worldwide, there are groups working to rectify pain, expose exploitation, combat torture, put right cruelty — all the things that 'they' seek to disguise. There is more morality, more desire for autonomy and individuality amongst men and women, especially women who are taking apart the halls of mirrors created by men, than Baudrillard, for some reason, wants to concede.

## Changing values

There may be a psychological need among some designers to elaborate their theories and provide complicated meanings as a framework for their work. Possibly some of them feel compromised by their role as servants to the manufacturers; the elaboration of meaning, of metaphors, is a way of justifying themselves creatively. One way of explaining away yet more excess and more consumption is to claim a contribution to the aesthetic qualities of life. Design, in all its elaborations, thus markets its own expansion on the grounds that it is doing good for the human spirit.

Designers and architects are especially good examples of people who depend upon elaborate justifications and meanings to give both purpose and structure to their work. Much of the technical justification is grounded in straightforward demands for safety, efficiency and economy, but the styles in which these technical ambitions are sought need more elaborate justifications. Sometimes the style, even in architecture, gets its meaning, its reason for existing, from marketing or corporate identity requirements. Occasionally, the ideology that justifies one style rather than another is more elaborate and designed to establish values that the style is intended to communicate to the wider public.

It is noticeable, for example, that product and furniture design in Denmark, Sweden, Finland and Norway has been shaped by social–democratic ideals – serving the comfort and safety of the human being has been an organizing principle in Scandinavian design, further enlarged, if we follow Baudrillard, by Scandinavians' self-perceptions of themselves as people who are concerned with design organized on social welfare principles. (Another aspect of the hall of mirrors is the way we live up to our own descriptions of ourselves – which is one reason why hypocrisy may perhaps be regarded as a tool of self-improvement.)

Yet, on the whole, the 1980s have been bereft of clear organizing principles and metaphors. Even the architects, masters of the elaborations of justifying frameworks, have been at sea – as the consumer objects they have designed have tended to show.

The revival of symbolism in architecture and in design has been argued for extensively by Charles Jencks, the American architect and theorist credited either with inventing or at least with popularizing the concept of post-modernism in architecture and design. Others, especially the American architect Robert Venturi, have contributed greatly to post-modernist design theory.

But Jencks seems particularly dogged by the problem of making his designs justifiable, giving them a purpose for existing via their symbolic meaning. His best-known effort in this regard is the interior of his Victorian London house, which he re-designed totally.

For a while I knew the house only through photographs. Then Jencks was kind enough to show me around. My general impression was that here was an essentially good-natured house: it is comfortable, idiosyncratic and outward going so long as you ignore some of the symbolism; if you don't, it became rather stressful.

The stress comes from the almost desperate way in which every *thing* has to have a 'meaning' in order that its existence can be justified. The symbolic interior becomes a metaphor of post-modern neurosis: if a thing has no meaning, it should not exist.

When one enters the house one does so through the 'Cosmic Oval' – the lobby is egg shaped (birth, beginning of the universe); around the ceiling is a frieze of faces, each face representing an important figure in history – Pythagoras, Hobbes and Jefferson are among those present. Aware of the potential absurdity of his pretensions Jencks attempts a little self-mockery with what he calls his 'cosmic-loo'.

Each room in the house has its theme – Winter, Spring, Summer, Autumn – and the themes are elaborated through decorated devices which have their roots in literary or fine art references. The virtue in all this rests in the fact that what Jencks strives for is a celebration of the positive aspects of human civilization; the interior is an acknowledgment of the fruits of scholarship, martyrdom, political striving and artistic endeavour.

None the less, for me the interior palls physically because Jencks has all the right ambitions for craftsmanship, decoration and design but the physical results seem disappointing. He will talk knowledgeably about how important it is that a room should be composed of different kinds of materials, how the designer must be alert to the different ways in which these materials reflect or defract light and how the light models a room. But Jencks' surfaces do not look very good. He or his craftsmen seem to lack the knowledge of and perception about materials – most of the surfaces are painted, there is relatively little use made of natural materials. (See also Chapter Six.)

The Jencks house fails for me because he has not demonstrated enough knowledge about crafts and craftmanship and because the ideas tend to be too literary; it fails also because it is neurotically over-labelled. Yet it is still significant: in seeking to establish a way in which design can be both innovative and still coherent, in searching out an approach which celebrates cultural achievements and innate human experiences

*A part of the Summer room in the London house of Charles Jencks and Maggie Keswick. The Sun chairs are made from layered planes of medium-density fibreboard.*

of the pleasures of the seasons, of conviviality and so forth, Charles Jencks has offered up an alternative to Baudrillard's post-modernist scepticism.

Jencks understands that the majority of people are still uneasy with the notion of useless objects that refer to nothing beyond what they are – a lot of modernist painting and sculpture is disturbing because of this meaninglessness. Of course, many more people can cope with the fact of a flower arrangement or a pretty stone picked from a beach not *meaning* anything other than what they are. But human-made artefacts which do not translate beyond themselves are upsetting. Sculpture is the more widely tolerated if it has the familiarity of form and relates to an event, a myth, a religious experience or is in some way representational.

There are, however, important and telling exceptions to this generalization. This chapter has spent some time on the aesthetic pleasure of the camera, stressing the fetishistic qualities of the camera as an object in its own right. And in one sense the formal pleasures that the amateur has in handling the camera are fairly close to the pleasures of a certain class of sculpture – and these are the pleasures of objecthood. Provided a thing has a function, however nominal or perfunctory, then sufficiency of meaning is enough to justify the object's existence. The justification is then set aside and the pleasures of the object itself enjoyed.

The sculptor William Tucker, in his essay 'The Object',[6] begins by saying: 'If one word captures the aspirations of modernism from about 1870 until the Second World War it is surely *object*.' And this objectness, of course, was sought not only in fine art but in design – indeed, it becomes a more powerful influence in industrial design only after the Second World War when the domestic consumer object becomes marketed as a thing for itself. The work of Dieter Rams (see Chapter Two) is the heritage of modernist sculpture; it brings modernist sculpture to the home and thus provides a certain kind of domestic art.

The search after objecthood in an object was, says Tucker, idealistic. It was a search for a classical entity, a search for clarity and for an absolute that was, like a scientific law, self-contained and independent of ego, of individual maker; and, therefore, it was conceived as being the best – it was not a compromise, not articulating anything other than what was thought to be beautiful.

One of the reasons why simple tools are so admired, even (especially) by those who do not use them, is the formal aesthetic, their self-containment. This is especially true of kitchen equipment; it hardly matters what the things are, for they excite interest because of their formal beauty.

Marcel Duchamp was excited by a bottle rack. William Tucker argues that Duchamp's sensibility was especially attuned to the formal integrity possessed by objects such as his famous 'readymades' (the bottle rack, snow shovel and hat rack). The integrity was typical of a great number of useful objects in general circulation from the 19th century onwards, objects in which economy and efficiency had been the only determinants of design.

Tucker enthuses: 'The abstract formal power of the bottle rack as a total configuration has not yet been equalled in sculpture....' (He wrote this in 1972 and – if some people have found it tendentious – it seems to me to define the success – and limitations – of modernist sculpture.)

One of the consequences of modernism's preoccupation with the search for aesthetic absolutes is, in retrospect, all too obvious. It makes change and it makes variety much harder to justify. If, for the sake of argument, you insist that this and only this range of forms, this and only this range of textures, is ideal (and all the rest are negated) then you end up with everything looking very similar. It happened with abstract art, it happened also with classical architecture. To put it bluntly, this *sameness* is literally bad for business. Products start looking alike and that makes competitive consumer capitalist enterprise very difficult – not only in manufacturing but also in art.

The key phrase 'product differentiation' is of interest to everyone who is in competitive enterprise, be they painters, sculptors, or manufacturers of cameras or electric hairdryers. Robert Blaich, managing director of industrial design at Philips, told Alix Freedman of the *Wall Street Journal*: 'So many products are the same today. You could take off the labels and you would not know *what company made them*'[7] (my italics).

And so one comes to the subject of product semantics, which is being pioneered in the United States. It refers to products that explain themselves as to what they are, what they do, and how they are to be operated. Perhaps the best examples of semantic products are indeed those of the 19th-century kitchen – a hand-operated whisk is about as obvious a machine as one can imagine (given, of course, some degree of familiarity with the material culture).

But designing self-explanatory, user-friendly objects in the late 20th century is made difficult by the use of electronics. The designer does not know what they do and has no immediate imagery with which to convey their function to the consumer. Gadgets that have wheels and gears and handles have an up-front logic about their working, but even if you tear the boxes off your computer, your telephone, your radio, TV, video, or fax machine and reveal the guts, those guts will be as meaningless to the majority of people as the internal anatomy of the human body was to early Renaissance anatomists.

There are, however, two issues here: the intention of designing self-explanatory functional objects is one discipline; product differentiation is another. Freedman's article in the *Wall Street Journal* made a revealing point of more significance to Europeans, perhaps, than North Americans. Michael S. McCoy of the Design Department, Cranbrook Academy of Art, is quoted as arguing, very cogently, that early attempts at 'expressive' design have not necessarily had much to do with a genuine expression of a machine. The big tail fins of the famous American cars of the 1950s suggested speed, suggested they were there to help keep the car in position on the road as you whooshed along. In fact, they had no scientific logic at all. Today, said McCoy, the new breed of automobile expresses good performance through the scientific styling of the body. But such cars (like Ford's Taurus) are still in a minority in the United States. They *look* different from the competition. In North-West Europe, where science and expression have fused in car design, the cars all look the same. That's the trouble with science and absolutes: one type of answer is generated. It is often a very expressive answer, but it fouls up the capitalist economy of competition. Car manufacturers in Europe have (at the point of writing) a major problem with product differentiation. Consequently there is a frenzy of different kinds of paint finishes, 'special edition' cars with fancy names and add-on graphics and sculpted wheel hubs. This is not quite the conspiracy it sounds, in so far as people enjoy being different (to a degree) and variety does freshen stale appetites. Nevertheless, differentiating between the various motives of the manufacturers and how far they want to satisfy existing desires as opposed to stimulating new ones, puts Baudrillard's scepticism about the unreality of the real in a sympathetic light.

Static objects, or objects that are simply carried around, and have solid-state electrical guts, are proving easier to deal with because the two intentions – being functionally expressive and looking different from the competitors – can be combined without loss of either design integrity or marketing chutzpah. Radios and stereos, for example, are not carrying human beings from place to place: as objects, they are not interfering mechanically with the world in the sense that is true of an automobile. There is no loss of function in making a radio or a stereo more sculpturally expressive, but there are potentially more losses in efficiency and even safety as soon as art begins to be applied to objects that interact in a mechanical way between a human being and the natural world.

Static or handheld objects give more freedom for symbolic interpretation or fashionable whim or marketing stylisms (and combinations of all three; the provenance of things, like that of ideas, is seldom from one source). Designers argue that in making a product expressive of its function one ought also to add a little wit, or provide a simile between the product and some other object (the most obvious example being Lisa Krohn and Tucker Viemeister's telephone in the shape of an address book, p. 28). Wit, expression and simile provide a good chance of making the product a bridge between two imaginations – that of the designer and that of the user. Objects that are imaginative bridges become, almost literally, poetic because poetry (as Philip Larkin once argued[8]) is about finding the appropriate metaphors to bridge from one human's experience to another's.

One of the examples that has most excited interest in the design world is a dot-matrix printer designed in 1987 by the American Lloyd Moore. Dot-matrix printers have, in the main, been ugly and horribly noisy. But, naturally, at first, one put up with the ugliness and the noise, indeed, hardly noticed them because, in the beginning, one was so impressed and pleased with the efficacy with which the new tool did its job: the combination of a micro-computer, a word-processing program and a dot-matrix printer revolutionized writing. The constant need for change and improvement, however, eventually asserted themselves; having got a machine that works, the next stage is 'how do we relate to it'.

Moore's printer is designed as a free-standing pedestal 'sculpture' redolent of the lectern or the pulpit and designed also to echo the way in which the print-out paper is scrolled. The design also captures, elegantly, the tough but light tautness and the insubstantial substantial-

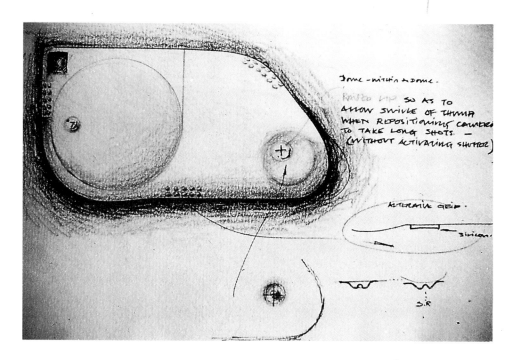

Drawings for a small camera by the designers Ross Lovegrove and Julian Brown
(UK). The aesthetic of modernist 'abstract' sculpture is married with the physical needs
of a user – the flattish, stone-like form makes the camera nice to hold and to use. The
similes do not shout at us.

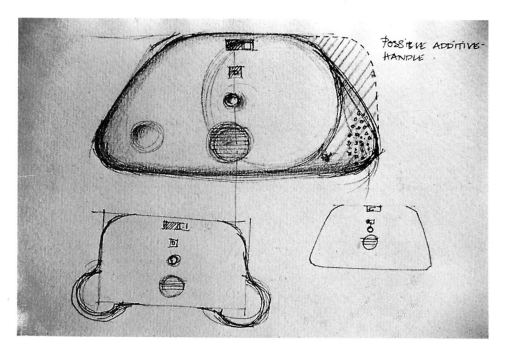

ity of paper. As a piece of design, it is deservedly award-winning. Curiously, bearing in mind that this object is claimed as a good piece of 'semantics', this printer has been given a name – it is called 'Elaine'. Is this expressive object in fact an example of the thinking Forty, Hardyment and others have criticized with regard to design for women in the home? After all, the 'Elaine' is intended to make the workplace brighter but who, most often, is the typist? A woman. And why call the thing 'Elaine'? This deluges the design with a lot of male assumptions and makes explicit a sexism that is otherwise usually hidden. Lovely Elaine, good to look at, good to feel, and a loyal worker. Let loose on this, the structuralists in the University literature departments around the world would have a field day.[9]

That said, it is a part of the designer's duty to improve the *person*-built material world in all its aspects – functionally and emotionally – and the Lloyd Moore printer, provided it is quiet, easy to maintain and reliably manufactured (it was not in manufacture at the time of writing), would be an improvement on much that is available.

The utilitarian argument for product semantics – making a thing easier to use – is unquestionably a good thing. In the design of a car interior, a railway locomotive cab, an aircraft cockpit, for example, the goal of self-explanatory design is a life-saving one. There is also, as has been discussed earlier, for example in the context of Jencks and symbolism, a need for our objects and surroundings to be given meaning in order to create some sense of purpose.

Some of the arguments marshalled into the post-modern/product semantic debate are a little risible, just as several of the younger generation of designers – with their desire to emote and express through their objects – are a little self-congratulatory. One doubts if the need for the symbolic design is always as pressing as some designers maintain. It is doubtful if people spend much time being confused by the similarity of form that exists between a microwave oven and a television set. A confusion over the controls of each item is a different matter. And a need to design tools that are child safe and usable by disabled persons or by the elderly is of continued importance.

The 'science' of product semantics (Professor Reinhart F.H. Butter, Ohio State University, says he and his team are looking at the subject in a systematic fashion in order to 'take the chance out of it') seems in danger of missing even bigger issues in design. For example, Bill Stumpf, whose work for Herman Miller is particularly well known, delivered a lecture in Amsterdam in 1987[10] in which he looked obliquely at the fashionable emphasis on metaphor in design.

Stumpf does not reject the role of metaphor in design; indeed, his work for Herman Miller pivots around ideas about domesticity, distraction and the idiosyncratic in the workplace. He does, however, believe that too much is produced that excludes the man or woman from interfering with the machine. He argued that it is becoming impossible for the owner to service his or her own equipment. He insists that things should work better than they do (see also pp. 145–6) and a part of that is being able to replace bits when they go wrong without the expense in time and effort spent taking it to a professional or calling one out. This kind of re-evaluation of design, of course, directly challenges the manufacturer's hegemony – an hegemony, a power, which depends on our disposing things which are 'apparently not worth repairing'.

There is the possibility that designers as stylists are simply replacing one kind of plastic box with another and demonstrating, yet again, the power of money (in the form of the big manufacturing combines) to change infinitely the face they present to the public while retaining control over the heart of their interests – manufacturing in bulk in a manner most convenient and profitable to themselves.

Stumpf, however, is subversive, whether intentionally or not, of something young designers cherish dearly – their own up-frontness. For it is clear that not only does product semantics differentiate the manufacturer, it also brings back the designer's ego. The quirkier the object, the more obvious an advertisement it is for the designer. For design is big, competitive business also. Stumpf is subversive of this attitude by implication. In the same Amsterdam lecture in which he explored the relationship between civility and design he said that comfort was a feature of civility and he defined comfort as an absence of irritation. Comfort reigns when you can take the infrastructure for granted; when it does not press itself upon you.

Should design be comfortable then? Not loud, but in the background. Serving but not irritating? Is up-front irritation best left to the artists?

# 5

# HIGH DESIGN

## The Lessons of Luxury

The challenges posed to ecology by consumerism *per se* are clearly the result of scale. On the whole, those who design and produce for the very rich are not likely to damage the world extensively in the process. The constituency of the rich is simply not that big. (Of course, the continued use of ivory, rare animal furs and exotic wood inlays are exceptions to this generalization.)

Designing for the very rich, however, poses an interesting headache for designers. For, if, as most of their clients appear to expect, designers are to create artefacts that look as though they are really expensive, luxurious and even unique, how are they to achieve these demanding objectives?

Even more intriguing is this: how do you devise objects that *are* worth a lot of money? For example, a meal costing 50 dollars can quite conceivably be a better meal than one costing 25 dollars. But is it possible that, costing 500 dollars, it will be 20 times better? Obviously beyond a certain – rather low – point, you begin paying for more than the raw necessity of decent nourishment. The rich, like the rest of us, are swiftly into the spiral of buying aspiration. But even with aspiration, at some point the designer's inventiveness palls and his or her ability to entertain runs out of steam. All that remains for the very rich to buy is nature or art or other people. Yet designers, retailers and the rich themselves keep on trying. The world of 'High Design' expands in an ever increasing effort both to exact profits from the rich and to maintain a distance of exclusivity and luxury from the rest of the consumer market.

The phrase 'High Design' is used here to cover two main categories of design and production in domestic or leisure products. These have been labelled *heavenly goods*; and *tokens*.

*Heavenly goods*: objects designed for the rich to buy
*Tokens*: objects bought by the 'wish-they-were-rich'

There are many examples of *heavenly* objects that can only be bought by the rich – handbuilt motor cars, America's Cup class boats and private aircraft are amongst the most visible. There is also a galaxy of very expensive versions of commonplace things such as luggage, clothes, accessories and knick-knacks. All are aimed at the international constituency of *the rich*. There are sub-divisions within this constituency, including the divide between old money and new money. New money, whose owners are still intoxicated with the novelty of the stuff, have provided a wealth of marketing opportunities and Nicholas Coleridge, in his book *The Fashion Conspiracy* (1988), notes some fairly desperate examples from the Dallas store Nieman–Marcus' annual matching 'His and Her' Christmas gifts:

| 1960: | His and Her Airplanes |
|---|---|
| 1962: | His and Her Chinese Junks |
| 1967: | His and Her Camels |
| 1970: | His and Her Thunderbirds |
| 1971: | His and Her Mummy Cases |

The habit continues today, but there are also many examples, such as the often beguiling *objets d'art* of Alessi, that are expensive but aimed as much at the professional classes with disposable income or access to overdrafts, as they are to the properly rich. Without implying criticism of Alessi (the point of singling them out is that many of their products are very desirable) one might observe that they have the same relationship between a discerning but relatively poor consumer that a museum shop has with a discerning but relatively poor connoisseur of art.

Visit a major museum, which today has a quasi-Church-like status (such as the Metropolitan Museum of Art in New York), and admire the treasures, which are about as accessible to you as things to own as the kingdom of heaven. But you can go to the museum shop and buy a relic, a token of what cannot be yours. Alessi 'knick-knacks' offer the same opportunity to buy a token of a world that you cannot really enter – that of the seriously rich.

In 1982 two American entrepreneurs, Addie Powell and Nan Swid, started a company in New York which organizes collections of tableware designed by well-known architects. Powell is recorded as saying that they are producing 'a status symbol at an affordable price'. One advertisement by one store said: 'Walk away with a Richard Meier original for considerably less than his normal fee.'[1] Both the Muséum of Modern Art in New York and the city's Metropolitan Museum of Art have samples from the Swid Powell collections.

The motive 'wanting to produce affordable status symbols' is not necessarily a bad one – there is a lack of generosity in sneering at people who want to have something to show off, especially when most of us like to have such things. Moreover, there is nothing which says that the notion of designing affordable status symbols leads to inferior design – it depends entirely upon where the designer starts.

For example, the BMW 316i motor car is an affordable status symbol; it is the lowest priced of the BMW range (admittedly *affordable* is a relative term but compared with a Rolls-Royce, Ferrari, Porsche – the most obvious status symbols among cars – the 316i speaks of the same kind of quality at a very much lower cost). The BMW has been described as feeling as if it had been carved from a piece of solid steel. You buy such a car and you are deemed not only to have taste but also to have bought wisely – it is a good product in its safety, its engineering and its finish. The designers have started out from the position of designing a good motor car whose perceived quality will flatter potential customers. Much packaging design, on the other hand, flatters the purchaser by promising him or her more than the object genuinely delivers.

There is another category or sub-category of high design which includes things such as handmade bicycles – bicycles that are built individually to the customer's requirements in order that the bike performs as well as any bike can for a specific task, say touring or hill racing. Other examples include specially built fishing rods, guns, bows and arrows for archery. What determines the constituency for this sort of object is not wealth *per se*, or even the desire to be associated with wealth, but the connoisseurship of a hobby taken seriously to the point of a passion. Thus a poor man or poor woman might save hard or go without in order to get the object that will best help him or her perform better in their hobby.

*Technology and marketing have created a style that proclaims 'culture' as well as 'money'. Now Museums are giving such objects a provenance which is lifting them towards 'art'.*

The key element in such things as good racing or touring bicycles is related to the primacy of the function. If the tool's performance is paramount then matters of metaphor, sensuousness, culture, marketing and bravado do not get much chance to enter the design or even the styling of the product. The specialist bicycle is such an example. Moreover, the quality of design, engineering and craftsmanship required to make a good functional bicycle put it into a class of its own.

Graham Vickers has written extensively about bicycle design and been critical of manufacturers and designers who have tried to *improve* on the basic bicycle concept. There have been some ingenious designs but, says Vickers, they are often clever solutions to self-imposed problems.

The heart of a good bicycle, whether for racing or pleasurable touring, is the frame. Vickers explains that the virtues are rigidity and lightness. The variables include the frame angles – and these are determined by the use to which the bicycle is to be put. 'Frame angles are varied to afford different handling characteristics . . . a 74 degree parallel frame with a 1 and a half inch fork rake gives a brisk response to power input and fast handling characteristics.' But such a configuration is uncomfortable over rough terrain, whereas 'angles of 71 or 72 degrees and fork rakes up to 2 and a half inches gives a better shock absorption but a more lethargic response.'

Naturally the craftsmanship is important. Vickers says: 'In the UK the small family business framebuilder is often operating very close to an economic nonsense – if he is still operating at all – and yet the traditional craftsman's pride in a job well done persists.'

In all categories of high design the concept of craftsmanship is important. Sailing boats are built by hand; leather luggage is often handbuilt; shoes, chocolates, sports equipment are made or finished by hand. Quite often hand building is the only economic way of proceeding. If the constituency for a product is small (but wealthy enough to pay a premium) then it is cheaper to use craftsmen and craftswomen than invest in very expensive 'intelligent' machines. In any case, it is being discovered that having a factory filled with very expensive intelligent machines demands a very expensive (albeit small) and intelligent workforce to keep it going.

But apart from economic necessity the presence of handworkmanship does declare the presence of a special kind of service. As David Pye has said (see pp. 144–7), much craft work involves the risk of failure, therefore the worker has to be specially attentive. Moreover, to build something well by hand (albeit using as many machines and jigs as can be afforded) does in fact necessitate values of selflessness – the craftsman is often working in one of a team, and there is a commitment to the product over and above the self-interest of the individual craftsman.

Nevertheless, and without seeking to imply that capitalism is bad for design, it is also the case that one of the underlying metaphors of high design, in addition to the virtuous ones of creating the best possible artefacts with the best possible skills, is the display of money.

## The Godhead of money

The first thing that becomes clear from examining how the wealthy operate and how the wealthy are served is that the rich provide a separate 'province' that ignores national boundaries. Retailers in London, Paris, New York and Milan know that the rich, whatever their nationality, have more in common with one another than with the poorer classes of their native countries. Lewis H. Lapham, American, editor of *Harpers* and author of *Money and Class in America* (published in 1988),[2] describes what it feels like to be rich, from the inside. He says you assume that the 'world will entertain you as its guest'. If you are rich the world is constantly smiling at you. Headwaiters are there to represent the world's opinion and 'their smiling respect confirmed a man in his definition of himself.'

Lapham argues that in the USA money can do anything and that it is an end in itself. The objects that one buys can never be elaborate enough to do full justice to the Godhead of money. He suggests that the very fact that a thing costs more adds to an American's belief in its efficacy: thus a $13 billion aircraft carrier has necessarily to be better than a $10 billion one. In the USA money has immense power: the very rich can buy the most dazzling 'objects' – 'it is difficult to think of anything in the United States that cannot be bought or sold – the presidency, a television network, longer life . . . a municipal judge, an ambassadorial post. . . . ' Whether the European rich are much more constrained in the things that they can buy with their money is a moot point. Europeans can buy television and newspaper networks and, undoubtedly, are adept at buying the circumstances that give them sufficient power to protect their part of the exclusive province.

According to Lapham, the possession of a lot of money makes the rich feel different about their own mortality. Dare God strike down the chief executives of Mobil Oil, IBM, the USA? And Lapham adds an interesting footnote: 'Precisely this superstition accounts for the continuing preoccupation with the sinking of the *Titanic*. Like the ship of which they were representative, the wealthy personages on board, among them an Astor and a Widener, were supposed to be invincible . . . Two days later, on April 17, 1912, the *Empress of Ireland* sunk in the Gulf of St. Lawrence, drowning 1,000 passengers. Nobody remembers the incident because the deceased belonged to an invisible and nonequestrian social class.'

The rich enjoy an ability to command surplus and unnecessary labour – two or three waiters at table, men or women hand stitching the leather upholstery on a car seat to go into a car that is itself built, laboriously, by

*A wealth of high performance, well-made consumer objects exists for the millions. Those who serve the rich rack their brains in search of 'exclusivity'. This Nikon camera is gold-plated.*

(Opposite) *Vase designed by Marcello Morandini (Italy, 1983) for the West German ceramics company Rosenthal. It is a limited edition knick-knack.*

hand. If a hamper of food is being sold for a picnic then it is important that the hamper itself be handmade. Exclusivity, which is what being rich enables one to enjoy, usually comes down to the ability to buy other people's service and servility.

This need not mean that the servile and the servants of the rich are necessarily over-exploited; they may earn good wages and enjoy esteem among their fellow crafts workers. They may also, because money is no object, relish the chance to exercise the best of their skills in the production of things for the rich.

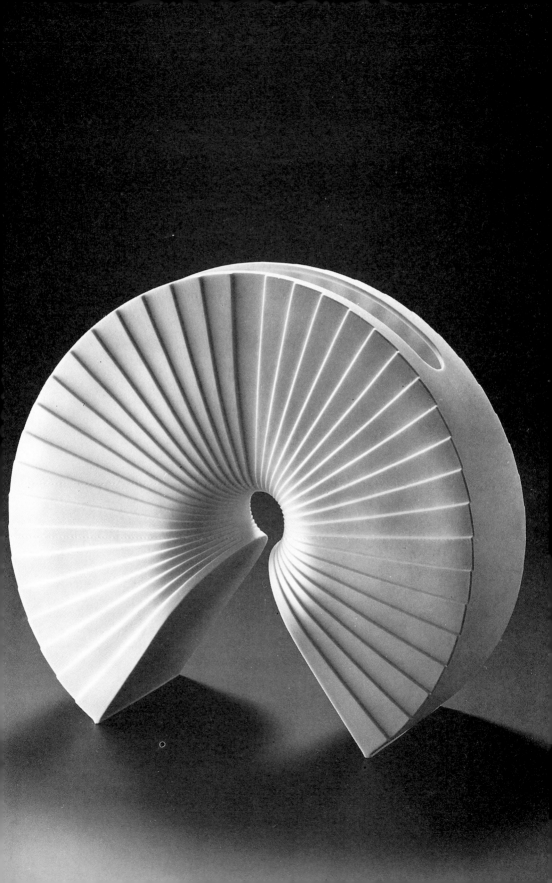

The power to have the exclusive rights to another person's labour is appealing because the possession of someone else's time is an absolute. All the other aspects of an object can be copied and mass produced and, horror of horrors, popularized.

This is what differentiates the 1980s from 1890, 1909, and even 1949 – the ability of industrial design and manufacturers to deliver goods that cannot be bettered, however much money you possess. The rich find their exclusivity continuously under threat.

There is an irony for the very rich in the Chairman of Aston Martin Lagonda, the exclusive car builders, being willing to say that a BMW is as well engineered as one of his own cars when the price differential can be as much as a $100,000. But then, in an age such as ours, which is so egregious in its ability to make things for the masses well (look at any Coke can) the differential of quality in the majority of objects is bound to be reduced to a relatively very small margin. This, ironically for socialism, is one of the successes of capitalism.

Beyond a certain, relatively low price (low compared with other times in history) the rich cannot buy a better camera, home computer, tea kettle, television or video recorder than you or I. What they can do, and what sophisticated retailers do, is add unnecessary 'stuff' to the object. You can have your camera gold plated, or the knob of the lid of the tea kettle made from ruby. You can, in other words, invent an exclusive product – as indeed some stores do. The design element is never innovative; what happens is that an existing design is given an exotic coat and an intimidating price. At Christmas 1988 Dunhill, one of the world's most sophisticated retailers to the rich with stores across the world, advertised under the heading 'The Craft of Giftmanship' – a motley of very expensive items such as an Ostrich Bill Fold, an Ostrich Hip Flask, a Thuya exotic veneered Humidor and a Champagne-face Millennium watch. Even the words are part of the added value – the champagne, for example, refers to the colour of the watch face.

## Heavenly objects

In Europe the best known of the heavenly objects that ooze both quality and exclusivity are motor vehicles. In 1988 Landor Associates conducted a survey about brand names in which there were two criteria: (a) the consumer's familiarity with the brand and (b) how good the consumer thought the product was. In Europe, the Rolls-Royce ranked 15th in terms of consumer familiarity, but 1st in terms of quality. Coca-Cola, on the other hand, the only brand in the world to be on all the world's tongue tips, was ranked 66th in Europe in terms of quality – presumably, as the *Economist* magazine commented, because people were worried about its sugar content.

Porsche is one of the names associated with the very rich and with quality. Most people know it through the Porsche motor vehicles. But there is also a separate Porsche design company whose studio is in Zell-am-See, in Austria. Its designs for companies such as Poltrona Frau (Italy), Artemide (Italy) and InterProfil (West Germany) include lighting, furniture and accessories. These accessories, such as hand luggage, sun glasses and smokers' pipes, are bought by the rich and the would-be rich. They are well made, precise and rigorous in their design – small objects of perfection that are their own advertisement for success and exclusivity. This design studio has also designed 'toys' that only the rich can afford, including an offshore motor yacht called the *Kineo*.

The *Kineo* is a design whose central metaphor is the machine aesthetic; it looks like the machine that only a man or a woman who owned an industrial combine could fully appreciate. It is like a visual summary of German efficiency, futurist obsession with speed, and the romance of pre-Second World War modernism. It is intimidating and aggressively phallic. Sexual connotations are too easily applied to high-technology design, but this object exudes a form of sexual aggressiveness that only the possession of good looks, wealth and youth could give you. It is an object from which to enjoy the world's smiles.

This is the description of the *Kineo* in the Porsche catalogue titled *Liberties and Limits* (1986/7): 'The unusual deck design of this power boat is based on purely ergonomic and functional criteria (especially the freedom of movement below deck) as well as aesthetic allusions to symbols of aggressiveness such as submarines and torpedoes. These functionally alien elements are incorporated stylistically.'

The message is aloof and challenging. It is interesting also to note the brand of exclusivity radiated by the catalogue, which displays intellectual elitism as well as the rarity of wealth. It is quasi-philosophical, quasi-intellectually rigorous – it is as though Kant has become chic, and

*For the person who can afford the* Kineo *motor yacht, such Porsche promotional assertions as 'Space has limits. So does liberty', are a reassuring comment on the legitimacy of privilege.*

Wittgenstein a designer–hero (which currently he is becoming[3]). At various points throughout the brochure statements and quotations are introduced. For example:

> Space has limits. So does liberty.
> Freedom may seem limitless but, of course, it isn't. As doctor and scholar Rudolf Virchow once said: 'Liberty is not the capriciousness of doing as one pleases but the ability to act reasonably.'

The ostensible reason for including these and other quotations in the catalogue is to suggest, without too much argument, the appropriateness of Porsche design. Porsche design is rooted in the pared down style of the Bauhaus. It uses apparent plainness as a metaphor for reason and logic. At the same time there are always a lot of embellishments which cannot be justified by reason (compare p. 146 and David Pye's

*Aston Martin Lagonda make fine, fast, hand-built sports cars. Ideally, an Aston Martin should be owned by a young male fairhaired English fighter pilot, heir to the Battle of Britain and the Spitfire.*

elaboration on the contradictions inherent in the usual 'form follows function' arguments). And so the references to freedom and limits to freedom are a nice way of arguing against post-modernism (as demonstrated by Graves), or excessively over-indulgent experimentation, while at the same time admitting that though Porsche design is rooted in the Bauhaus teachings, it does not strictly adhere to 'old-fashioned' modernist dogma.

But what is also significant is the political presumption of these remarks; they are addressed not to mere consumers but to the educated 'equestrian' class who run things, for whom a debate about limits is more than philosophical speculation – it is of practical interest. It is almost as if the metaphors employed by Porsche design suggest a hidden agenda – a design that articulates power, control and domination in the same way that equestrian statues or paintings have done through the centuries.

In Aston Martin, a British design, the visual metaphors are similar — the Aston Martin V8 and V8 Vantage Volante are big and aggressive vehicles. However, the hidden metaphors are in the making. The Aston Martin Lagonda automobile company makes the only hand-built, as distinct from hand-assembled, car in the world. There are some luxury cars of quality, assembled by hand from machine-pressed or machine-made parts. At Aston Martin the chassis and the body are hand formed around formers and shaped by being pummelled around these formers by craftsmen body bashers wielding mallets. A large amount of the engine (which is assembled by hand) is machined inhouse from rough castings supplied by a sub-contractor. Gear boxes, final drive units and electrical fittings are also supplied from outside — handmaking a light bulb would be unusually idiosyncratic even by British standards.

You can, if you wish, visit the factory and watch your car being built. You will then be able to enjoy more richly the pleasures of men working with such rare skills especially for you. The experience is not, of course, cheap.

## Serving the rich with handmade artefacts

It would be wrong to think of the craftsmen or craftswomen who are involved in the creation of expensive, one-off artefacts for the rich as necessarily subservient; they are certainly not exploited. Indeed, the creation of an artefact by a team of highly skilled people working for someone else is complex and as an act of working involves values that can be profound. Thus I want to explore in more detail the creation of another sort of 'heavenly object' — the modern tapestry.

There is a thriving business turning paintings into tapestries for the rich, with painters as various as Helen Frankenthaler (USA), David Hockney (UK/USA), Sir Eduardo Paolozzi (UK) and Frank Stella (USA) having their paintings turned to tapestry. Why? And why, such eminent artists notwithstanding, would it be especially surprising if instead a Georg Baselitz was so transformed?

All the painters above, and more besides, have had their work translated by the Edinburgh Tapestry Company, one of the world's few tapestry companies.[4] PepsiCola, for example, commissioned from them a suite of eleven tapestries, each one based on an illustration by Frank Stella.

Tapestry differs from painting because its structured and constructed surface relates more easily and naturally with other manmade or wrought surfaces in a room. Whereas a painting, it is argued, is an environment on its own – it refers to itself, not the other objects in the room.[5]

The effects of the refraction and reflection of light are also different. Light is reflected off the non-porous surface of paint, but with yarn more of the light is absorbed and it bounces around inside. The colour is thus enlivened and as a result tapestry can be a very rich medium. The coarseness, the type of yarn used and the density of the warp per inch will each determine the nature of the texture and by altering the texture you can, literally, model with light.

The dynamics of the textile surface and the enriched colour excite painters. At the Edinburgh Company the managing director, James More, explained how he and his colleagues spend time talking with the artist, going through the work and discussing possible images for turning into tapestries. Naturally, they like to live through an artist's work for a while.

When an image has been chosen a cartoon is made and the threads of the warp on the loom are impressed with an ink copy. The weavers follow the ink marks as their guides as they inch their way along and up the image. The first quarter of the tapestry is crucial because this determines the range of the hues, tones and textures for the rest of the composition. Unlike painting, tapestry is not a medium that you work all over as you progress. On the contrary, it is a step-by-step linear route – like moving up a mountain. At Edinburgh, three to four weavers work on a tapestry together; they are 'chained' together by a consensus which, with constant reference back to the artist's original work, stops them from falling apart.

The weavers insist they are translating, not copying. They abhor a slavish rendering of a painted image. The use of analogous textures and the creation of colour is, obviously, crucial. It is understood that at the Gobelins works in France there are yarns in 17,000 different hues, but the Edinburgh Company stocks around 1,500. The weavers must mix yarns and, with the combination of three or four variously coloured yarns loosely or tightly entwined together, subtle gradations and nuances are possible. The technique of colour mixing in tapestry is to an extent *pointillist*.

The thinking involved in translating a Frankenthaler or a Stella into a tapestry lies somewhere in between the two extremes of copying and invention. On the one hand, the weavers are following someone else's thinking; on the other, they are having to do some interpretation in the creation of the tapestry.

But there is another aspect to the thinking involved.

When a painter paints it is clear that the surface resulting from his or her brush strokes is due as much to the accidents as to the painter's conscious decision making. For example, if you lay down a colour and then scumble another colour over it – half-covering it – then it cannot be claimed that you chose every centimetre of the resultant effect *before* you painted or even *as* you painted. You might like the overall result and decide to leave it but you did not decide every visible juxtaposition of grain to grain. Yet the master weaver, when re-creating in weave that scumbled area, has to think through everything the painter was able to 'dash' off. The weaver turns every one of the painter's 'accidents' into deliberations. He or she re-works the effects that were caused initially by the speed of a painter's brush, gravity, the consistency of the paint and the room temperature. This is one reason why tapestries tend to have a slightly stilted air; they are not fluid artefacts.

And in fact, despite the argument that this is translation, not copying, the Edinburgh weavers keep faith with the scumbles, the drips, the broken line and the overlays. It appears to be intelligent, interpretative work, true, with, none the less, copying at its heart. The tapestry does not, indeed cannot, seek to make itself indistinguishable from the original painting – the one is not a facsimile of the other but nor is the painting only a sketch for the tapestry. On the contrary the painter's thinking, choices, perception provide most of the tapestry craftsperson's universe.

The master weavers demonstrate substantial skill and the demonstration of virtuoso skill in today's fine art is rare. The skills include:

— a deep understanding of colour
— an ability to interpret texture
— a feeling for line
— very good observational skills

None of these skills are learned by rote; they each demand a combination of experience, learning and intuition. They demand both intelligence and the gift of emotionally sympathetic imagination that enables the craftsperson to put himself or herself in the artist's place. The master weavers are not without ego but their goal is a communal one – to do right by the spirit of the original artwork. Thus, in the best sense of the word, they are servants to the painting and equal collaborators with the painter. They have achieved this equality, not by becoming artists, but through the rigour of their skill and their service. Once it is decided by the artist that he or she wants a work translated into tapestry, then he or she is in the hands, eyes and imagination of the craftsperson.

And this is an equality achieved through having different roles.

Yet, on the whole, contemporary fashion is against craft, against the virtuosity of skill – it is regarded as second-class knowledge. Whatever other merits they have, the paintings of Julian Schnabel or Georg Baselitz cannot claim much in the way of virtuoso skills.

The types of painting favoured as material for tapestries fall into one or both of two categories: optimism and decoration. A David Hockney painting tends to be both optimistic and decorative – his representations of effects of light on objects, his paintings with flowers or incidental domestic still lives have the poignancy of a moment caught on the turn.

Other works, such as those by Frank Stella or Helen Frankenthaler, are certainly decorative and also non-subversive. A lot of abstract paintings, irrespective of the theories that have packaged their arrival as art commodities, are glorified extensions of wallpaper – and none the worse for that.

Tapestry is itself a decorative art. A tapestry is an object which relates to and fits in with other objects – it is a wall furnishing. But the appropriateness of turning a Hockney or a Stella into a tapestry and the inappropriateness of effecting the same transformation upon a Baselitz has slightly deeper roots.

Making a tapestry is a positive thing – it comes about from a huge human commitment: years of learning techniques, then hundreds, possibly thousands of hours spent on the construction of a single tapestry. Such a commitment in time and skill betrays a belief in the innate value of the object as a thing worth producing. It is therefore a wholly inappropriate medium for the subversive gesture, for the anti-art statement, or a fashionable two fingers to the bourgeoisie. To commit a Baselitz to tapestry would be to clash two incompatible value systems together. The communal quiet, constructive and painstaking work of the master weavers – men and women whom you would trust to take care in other aspects of life – has no meeting point with an ego that disavows care, attention and scrupulousness. It would also drain from the Baselitz the one clear thing it has going for it: an immediacy which directly connects the viewer with the artist's physical gesture.

By implication, of course, one can re-address the values of decorative art, which can often include the demonstration of skill and the aim of serving to please. The importance of the communal appeal of skill is taken up in the next chapter.

So why do people buy Stella tapestries? Since the mid-1950s large abstract paintings have had a good track record in attracting corporate clients; big and colourful, and often with an anonymous subject matter, these abstractions fit in well with other contemporary artefacts such as Barcelona chairs.

Tapestries can be better: client and viewers can see the value for money in the excess of skill and hand labour. As investments, tapestries have the advantage that even if people hate the imagery they must acknowledge the skill. The company accountant can cost what he or she has bought in terms of real hours per dollars per inch. A tapestry provides a lot of materiality for a material world.

Even better is the combination of the rich and virtuous substantiality of tapestry with the provenance of an established artist. Hence the Stella *Had Gadya* tapestries for PepsiCola, complete with a very well-designed catalogue to explain the provenance of (i) the PepsiCola Collection; (ii) Frank Stella; (iii) the Edinburgh Tapestry Company; and (iv) the illustrations for the tapestries.

Stella is presented as the innovator; the tapestry weavers, rightly, as the master craftsmen. But, just in case anyone thinks Stella is winging it solo, his own work is given art historical provenance. We are told that this suite is based both on Russian constructivist imagery and the Passover parable song *Had Gadya*. The Edinburgh weavers' pedigree is soundly rooted in William Morris's studio at Merton Abbey.

Tapestries have other qualities, such as durability. A modern tapestry will almost certainly last 500 years, paintings not yet a tenth of that are causing headaches for conservationists. They also have practical benefits such as softening the acoustics of a hall.

And, most important of all, they are pleasant furnishings. They are warm and they are positive – their positiveness being woven into them. In general, carefully crafted objects might be moving, they might be kitsch – but they are seldom, if ever, cynical.

On the whole high design, especially in the art/craft area just discussed, is conservative, not subversive. This is, in part, a consequence of the fact that such work tends to be commissioned. Very few people or institutions are going to commission work that threatens or subverts their own values.

There is a distinction between unnecessary labour as executed by servants or traditional or quasi-traditional craftsmen and *artist*-craftsmen. The craftsmanship that the rich favour is designed to please them, not the craftsmen. The 'artist' or 'designer-craftsman' discussed in the next chapter is altogether too independent to be considered in the category of high design. The crafts bought by the rich are conformist, conservative and clearly following the whim of the client and not any creative exploration on the part of the craftsman. High design is conservative because although the members of the constituency of the rich want to appear different from the poor, they want, none the less, to be seen to belong to their own group. After all, one of the common denominators in society is the fact that nearly everyone wants to belong to some class or group; a function of material objects is to signify this belonging.

## Tokens

Some of the objects under consideration are brand names that will be known locally in countries of Europe or states within the USA amongst the professional classes, the would-be-rich, the aspiring, design (and therefore status) watching young. Among these brand-named objects are Mont Blanc, Bang & Olufsen, Bodum, the Panasonic pocket television, the hand-held Copy Jack 96 pocket copier, and the Braun shaver.

The 1980s upsurge in 'Design' as an activity to participate in, buy into, watch or discuss appears to parallel the similar upsurge in interest in fine art that occurred in the 1960s and 1970s. Then fine art was turned into a mass commodity via tens of thousands of books, millions of postcards, aggressive curating and rampant, albeit antagonistic coverage in newspapers and magazines. There was even a time around the early 1970s when there was the slogan: 'Everyone is an artist'. Design has not gone quite that far.

Design has, however, arrived as a serious cultural 'object' in its own right. Just as a piece of art now carries with it the possibility that it, or something similar, could be put into a museum and thus taken seriously as a profound example of contemporary culture, so too does design. In the past the commonplace objects of everyday use seldom ended up in a museum but today, provided the provenance is fashionable, all manner of designerly objects – typewriters, electric shavers, tea kettles, microcomputers, pocket televisions, pens – are collected, put on exhibition, curated, catalogued, classified and eulogized. Design is not only commerce, not only about the here and now but, thanks to the museum culture, it is also culture, also timeless, also *classical* – the favourite word of praise.

Most people, hitherto, could never have dreamed of owning objects with such a status.

Consider: museums collect and display the *same* goods that are featured in glossy magazines and written about by pundits. And, if you are sharp enough, you can buy the very same things yourself: the presence of so much official as well as media provenance for Graves's Alessi tea kettle, the Mont Blanc pen, the Copy Jack 96 pocket copier turns the object into a metaphor of itself. You buy one of these things and you buy directly into something much bigger – official contemporary culture.

There is the privilege of owning a thing that you can see pictured in the best settings and collected by the best people. And this privilege is a bonus added to the fact that the object, certainly those named, are in themselves well made, well designed and – in their own functional as well as aesthetic terms – a *good* thing.

Here we have another aspect of the desirability of these tokens. Consumerism is fed, made exciting and glamorous and enticing by advertising. Advertising and promotional gambits create expectations, but especially in the past these were, mostly, illusory. The actual objects could not deliver the fulfilment demanded of them, partly because the expectations were in themselves separate 'objects' – objects of the imagination which therefore existed only in the minds of the individual

consumers. Some of the products of late twentieth-century manufacturing, on the other hand, come as close to the perfection of form, touch
and operation as is possible and, moreover, they at least fulfil all the
material expectations announced in the advertisements. They do not
change your life, but increasingly the source of disappointment is not in
the product itself. Hitherto it was thought that only the rich could afford
to buy the kinds of things that did not disappoint you. As has been said
earlier, one of technology's increasing successes is the provision of a
democracy of excellence.

The quality of design has benefited and is benefiting from this curious
cultural packaging. A lot of talent is involved in making all kinds of
objects, however 'commonplace', not only well designed but also
beautiful. Cutlery, door handles, typewriters, watches and pens are
among them. The fact that the stuff is collected, written about,
discussed, pored over and debated, the fact that there is recognized to be
an iconography in design, a vocabulary, a concatenation of shared
meanings, has brought a seriousness to the subject and to mass
manufacture that is different in scale and depth of research to anything,
including the Bauhaus, that has preceded it.

Scepticism, of course, abounds. At the end of 1987 America's *Spy*
magazine ran an article about design, which it called *Yuppy Porn*. The
introduction nearly says it all:

It's compact. It's synthetic. It's very quiet.
It's hard but may be rubbery to the touch.
It's black or white or gray or silver.
It was designed by Germans or Italians, or people who wish they were
   German or Italian.
It's probably electronic, maybe digital.
It didn't exist when we were children.
Its quality is high – higher than we need.
It's not a necessity. It needs explaining.
It was not cheap.
We felt a little silly and excited buying it.
We feel a little guilty and proud showing it off.

The article argues, and who would deny it, that these objects are worn as
badges to confirm the status of their owners. (They are also signs of

belonging. You may be prompted out of rivalry and envy to want to compete with your friends through buying high design objects, but wanting to be seen to belong is perfectly understandable and, in a sense, it is the flip side of rivalry.)

There is another twist as well: in so far as advertising is adult fairy-tale telling there is something unsettling in the notion that the characters in the advertisements – the lovely objects – can become real, take off from the page or the TV screen and into your hands. The fantasy and the real object become one. It gets worse than that. Most of the objects listed above have no necessity about them; they were conceived, not to serve but to titillate. They are themselves objects of fancy. And so their creation, promotion, acquisition and lauding becomes a most strange exercise in contrived stimulation and satisfaction. It is here that the metaphor of 'pornography' might apply.

But the equation of high design and decoration (for these things are a modern version of an applied art) with pornography seems too much of a conceit. Pornography seems to be a private, introverted activity – its vocabulary may be shared, but its objects are furtive. The world of pornography hardly seems to have room for 'courtesy', 'charm', 'wit' or 'delight' – these are concepts which have implicit in their meaning the notions of 'sharing' and 'communality'. Design is based on sharing: it is a communal activity, its goals are communal – it seeks not the furtive satisfaction of the private individual but public pleasures of many individuals.

In Europe designers such as George Sowden (UK/Italy) and Matteo Thun (Austria/Italy) are committed to a design approach that is fashionable, trendy and even yuppy, but also celebratory and good natured – it is well intended.

Neither of them believe in the orthodox market-research orientated approach to product design. Thun and Sowden do not design to the preconceptions of salesmen. Both of them also mock, albeit gently, the efficient, market-related reductivist approach of the West Germans. They distance themselves from the quasi-Bauhaus aesthetic that is held to characterize Braun. Indeed, Thun goes so far as to deny that he is a product designer at all: 'I am an architect. I am not an industrial or a product designer of the West German mode. The approaches are quite different. It is not a question of being "better" but it is like trying to compare wine with cola.' Thun's goal is that his work should promote

*George Sowden designed this stainless steel coffee pot for Bodum in 1987. Sowden exploits advanced manufacturing methods to produce decorative design at a reasonable price. The domain of the handcraftsperson continues to shrink.*

or sustain 'well-being', while George Sowden wants to take the violence out of design: 'I want objects that make me feel happy, secure. In the 1970s product design was full of violence . . . even the telephones looked as though they were about to accelerate like Concorde.'

Sowden, like Thun, trained as an architect. In his design partnership with Nathalie du Pasquier he revels in the catholicity of his work – he has designed shoes, carpets, clocks, furniture and computer keyboards. His work for Bodum is especially interesting because it uses advanced technology to mimic craft results. The coffee jug, fruit bowls and glass holders designed by Sowden for Bodum are made from stainless steel. The metal is perforated and cut whilst it is flat, using a scanner to read the design and a laser cutter to make the perforated decoration. The range of decoration possible is broad and it is economic to produce a few of one design and a few of another. Sowden says: 'You are making something that until recently could only be made by handcraft techniques but which is now done by machine. And this means that to talk of a *machine* aesthetic no longer makes sense.' It also muddies the concept of the *craft* aesthetic. However, the polishing of these Bodum products is done by hand and that is the most expensive part of the process.

The richest part of Sowden's aesthetic lies in the decoration he uses to embellish or penetrate the surface; Matteo Thun seeks to communicate with the forms, not pattern. Taking a teapot he had designed, Thun said: 'Look. Here the handle is a verandah, a balcony. The lid is the roof, the base is the basement. Here is the first floor.' And then, of a tea tray: 'The handle is like a bridge. With a bridge you walk between two points. You lean over. You watch.'

Both Thun and Sowden have attempted a synthesis between the perfection possible via the machine and the potentially anarchic intervention of the artist or the designer or craftsman. They have pursued a design aesthetic that is intended to be reassuring, non-subversive, disposing its user and purchaser to security and well-being. It has a courteous charm; it also reflects the day-to-day appearances of contemporary life – it takes the surface marks of modern materials, city scapes and electronic technology and turns them into a non-nostalgic abstract decoration.

Courteous design, together with cultural provenance of the design and high-quality manufacturing, are embracing class after class of object. The West German manufacturer FSB, which makes door

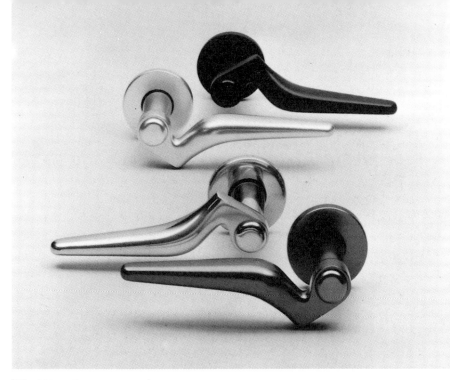

*The West German manufacturer FSB organized a competition for some of the world's leading architects and designers to produce a range of door handles. The handles here are by Hans Hollein (Austria).*

handles, has employed some of the key European architects and designers to revitalize its range: Alessandro Mendini, Dieter Rams, Mario Botta and Hans Hollein among them. From America FSB brought in Peter Eisenman and from Japan Shoji Hayashiu and Arata Isozaki. These men and others were brought together in 1986 for a 'workshop conference' to discuss with FSB the philosophy of design and the application of that philosophy to door handles.

When the time came to launch the product ranges, FSB released a catalogue/book which documents the conference. Called *Door Handles – Workshop in Brakel*, this publication provides an intellectual and cultural provenance which lifts the humble door handle into a fully idealized cultural object. It is a fascinating multi-layered gambit because (a) the association with such important names and with such culture is good marketing; (b) the seriousness with which the company is seen to pursue design is also good marketing; (c) the marketing has a solid base because, very probably, the designs *really* are good. FSB exists to earn money, but does so through good products. Furthermore, it is legitimate to argue that attention to all physical and material details goes a long way to making the world feel better. Nice door handles have their place.

The example of people arguing about door handles also has its funny side and the catalogue contains fine examples of national stereotypes: the very logical West German Dieter Rams is here on record as seeing the process of design in terms of an equilateral triangle; the Italian designer Mendini begs to differ – it is a labyrinth; while American Peter Eisenman talks fervently of 'real' and 'authentic' experiences.

Another example concerns the West German ceramics manufacturer Rosenthal which has commissioned, among others, the American ceramicist and textile designer, Dorothy Hafner. She has a well-established reputation within the American crafts community and has worked with Tiffany and Co. Like George Sowden, her particular talent is for surface decoration.

The cultural packaging that tends to accompany talented work such as hers is interesting. In 1987 a travelling exhibition organized by the Museum Het Kruithuis in Holland presented some of her work, and an American art critic, John Perreault, wrote an essay which is a fine example of how willing 'high culture' is to become a form of marketing. We have already noted the Porsche catalogue, with its appropriation of philosophical and political rubrics which it has applied like decals to add conceptual decoration to its products, and noted also the workshop–conference of FSB. And in England, the hugely successful advertising agency Saatchi and Saatchi has been known to preface its annual reports with erudite essays in support of the moral worthiness of advertising[6] – one essay took its cue from some lines in Shakespeare's *King Lear*. But in this essay, by John Perreault, the cultural packaging is even more transparent.

For example, in the context of Hafner's work, Perreault poses not a scholarly question, but an advertiser's gambit: 'Which is better as art? The large painting destined for imprisonment in a big city museum where it can only be seen during certain hours and after the viewer has paid an entrance fee? Or the table setting that one can be in contact with every day? The plate, the cup and saucer, the serving dish that can be touched and lifted as well as looked at?'

Well, obviously, we know what the answer is going to be in this context. Give us the dinner plates! All the 'essay' required to make it an advertising feature is one of those forms familiar to British and

American readers shouting at you to set down your credit card number: '*YES* – rush me my exclusive Hafner dining suite now!!!'

Generality, the weakness of Perreault's essay, is also its strength. For, if we do not pause over the phrase 'The large painting', we will not stop to wonder which of the large number of large paintings we are supposed to have in mind. Something by Jackson Pollock? Or Gustav Courbet or Titian or Balthus? Are all large paintings of equivalent value and content? Admirable though Hafner's work is, it is probable that she would be the first to say there was no contest if the choice is between her plates and, say, a Courbet. I suspect that Perreault has only large *modern* paintings in mind for the reason that so many of these are no more (and no less) profound than a dinner service.

Perreault wants his argument to pivot on the concept of ownership. And it is the concept of individual ownership that characterizes consumerism and design. Ownership has become a value and end in itself. In consumerist terms it matters very much that you can handle, touch, caress and gaze at a thing that is *yours*. But that is a necessary characteristic of consumer design. It is not a characteristic of profound art. It matters not one whit whether you own the Vermeer you are staring at or the limewood altarpiece by the German, Tilman Riemenschneider. Your imaginative relationship with the work or your understanding of its spiritual or empirical content is not affected by your not owning the work.

Design, however, is intended and marketed differently. It is intended to be sold and to be consumed individually. It just happens that one of the tactics of modern marketing is to seek to elevate such objects into art by comparing them with art and, of course, as already noted, converting them into the full currency of culture by having them displayed in museums.

Judging by Perreault's argument, and he is not alone, to make the strategy work it seems that one has to pretend that there is no hierarchy in art. If we can assert that the choice is not between the profound and the commonplace, but between 'art' that is in museums and 'art' that is in the home then we convey the impression that a dinner plate is equivalent to any other artistic endeavour. A pretended equivalence, a democracy of 'art' objects, is a useful strategy in the marketing of design as high design.

# 6

# VALUING THE HANDMADE

## Studio Crafts and the Meaning of their Style

One of the arguments in the previous chapter was that the term 'handcrafted' is potent because it implies a relationship of power between the purchaser and the maker. This relationship is traditional; it is the age-old one in which the client expresses his or her financial (and 'moral') superiority over others by exercizing his ability to buy unnecessary labour. Another, not quite contradictory but none the less temporizing argument, concerned the ability of craftsmen and craftswomen to work in teams with an artist or lead designer willingly and enthusiastically putting the integrity of the group project beyond their own creative self-expression.

But in this chapter the subject is different. We consider the work and the social role of another sort of craftsperson whose work, although apparently traditional, is in fact a thoroughly 20th-century invention. This is the work of the middle-class artist or designer-craftsperson, sometimes called the studio craftsperson. Here the starting point is with the creative fulfilment and self-expression of the individual craftsperson who works first to his or her own designs, not those of the client or an overseeing artist or designer.

The central discussion thus pivots around the individual maker, not the client, though – naturally – the role of the consumer of studio crafts is of relevance and interest. Crafts activity is intriguing: it is a somewhat artificial activity, but its virtues include the provision of alternative aesthetics to those offered by industrial design and the provision of a way of life that offers a protection against the sometimes overwhelming 'realities' presented by late 20th-century scepticism. The crafts are one of a number of popular strategies by which intelligent men and women have turned back from the shore of scepticism and into the warm sea of belief.

The chapter begins with a brief account of the work and ideas of Professor David Pye. The values he has described in his books and demonstrated in his own craft as a wood turner and carver are central to the ideology of mainstream modern craft. He is also useful because his ideas span both handicraft and industrial design. A brief overview follows, to provide a general picture of the studio craft scene.

I then discuss the ways in which contemporary craft is a 20th-century invention, and discuss the positive roles of what I have termed 'conservative craft'. The role of craft as a bundle of alternative aesthetics concludes the chapter.

## David Pye

I sometimes carry a small round wooden box. It fits comfortably in a pocket. The box is the sort of handcarved artefact that delights many people with its pretty demonstration of intelligent skill. The lid top has a sharp striated pattern whose finely cut ridges glitter and make whorls in the light as you screw the lid off away from the box. Around the edge of the lid is a piece of fine beading: it sits proud of the surface with cleanliness; it is not slurped in profile where it meets the base of the lid, not like a slumped serif on a poorly drawn letter.

There is pleasure in the tightness of the pull of the lid away from the container and, inside, the wood is clean and dark and neat. The body of the box exudes a mellowness because light is in part reflected and part absorbed by the gently oiled kingwood, which is faintly purple in its general chestnut colour.

The box is tiny, and pretty useless except for keeping tiny objects in, but it is a lesson in the possibilities of surface treatment and a reminder of the very special value of human skill.

Demonstrations of virtuoso skill are of great value for their own sake. We do not need to justify or explain our delight in watching and listening to a brilliant violinist; similarly, we can take pleasure in the physical evidence that demonstrates how a person's mind, eye and hand has produced, against so many odds, a piece of fine work. What we admire is the delivery of beauty in the teeth of risk. At the heart of the workmanship of risk is the thrill of avoiding failure.

David Pye made this box. Pye was born in 1914. He trained as an architect at the Architectural Association, London, and until he joined the navy in the Second World War he specialized in the design of wooden buildings. After the war he was invited to teach in the school of Furniture Design at the Royal College of Art, London, where he became Professor of Furniture Design in 1963. He retired in 1974. In 1968 he published *The Nature and Art of Workmanship*, and in 1978 *The Nature and Aesthetics of Design*.

There are four areas in which Pye's influence as a craftsman, writer and teacher is proving to be seminal: he has organized our ideas as to the nature of skill and the actual, rather than the assumed, differences between the process of bulk manufacture and that of single or limited production. He has challenged at a practical and at a philosophical level our conceptions about function and utility. He has directed attention to the importance of surface and surfaces. He has at all times kept his mind, and the minds of his pupils or readers, on the trilogy that necessarily shapes any design – namely, the scientific properties of the material, the knowledge of the craftsman (who could be a female product engineer), and the qualities we seek in order to be civilized.

But if, excepting his boxes and carved wooden bowls, David Pye was remembered for only one thing, then it would be for his distinction between the workmanship of *risk* and that of the workmanship of *certainty*.

Take, as an example, writing longhand with a pen. There is always the threat of blotting the paper or of your hand slipping as you write – this is the workmanship of risk. Likewise when we watch the violinist and marvel at the dexterity, we also admire the courage that confronts the possibility of failure. With the workmanship of certainty, however, once the process of manufacture has been set up, the results are predictable: if 'x', then necessarily 'y'.

None the less, Pye points out, within the workmanship of certainty, there will have been a history of risk – the jigs and the machines (and now, the computer software) that provide the certainty were themselves brought into being by varying degrees of trial and error. Conversely, most workmen who rely on the relationship between their hands and their brains – whether making furniture, clay pots or body panels for an exotic sports car – devise all kinds of machines to limit their risk.

*David Pye, writer, designer and craftsman, is famous for the finesse of his carved and turned wooden boxes. He is a master of the wooden surface. He has remarked that many people's knowledge of surface has atrophied through their reliance on photographs rather than an empirical scrutiny of the thing itself.*

The commercial usefulness of the workmanship of risk is constantly being reduced in mature industries as manufacturers seek more refinements to reduce failures. Even so, in large, initially one-off projects, such as the construction of nuclear power plants, the workmanship of risk is of value because much of the work is new – the design exists, but getting it made for the first time involves problem solving. Much will not have been predicted by the engineers.

The elegance of the risk/certainty distinction rests in its removal of the false opposition of the hand versus the machine – it establishes that using or not using a machine is a red herring. The critical characteristic that distinguishes one kind of workmanship from another is at what stage creative choice is introduced into manufacture.

Pye punctures received opinions. In *The Nature and Aesthetics of Design*, he cut open an embarrassing contradiction in the rubric of 'form follows function' (a rubric that still has an emotional appeal). He establishes that the designer has more freedom over the form than over the function, thus standing on its head the one modernist principle that was held inviolate. He argues (a) that the ability of our devices to work and give results depends much less exactly on their shape than we think (even a pair of 'identical' ball bearings differ from one another and each is not, in any case, spherical); and (b) that all our devices are prone to function in ways that we do not want. Car tyres wear out, table tops get scratched, knives lose their edge, aircraft crash.

More and more debate about design has turned into a debate analogous to literary criticism; we ask ourselves 'what does a design mean' and not 'what does it do'. And in concentrating on meaning we lose ourselves in words; the actual object is left behind, and it escapes a proper audit on matters such as how well it wears, what it feels like, even how safe it is. 'Purpose' exists in men's minds, 'results' exist in things. Pye says it is better to found a practice of design on results, not a theory based around intentions.

Half teasing, Pye reckons that we spend a lot of time embellishing things to make up for the fact they do not work well enough. Only half teasingly, though, because he has also remarked: 'To say of a design "it works" no more commends or excuses it than to say of a man "he has never actually defrauded anybody".' He knows that, functionally, all kinds of 'lash-ups' will work, will make do, but he actually seeks a world in which the surfaces we work are imbued with skill and imaginative good manners.

Surfaces are everything to Pye because surfaces are all we actually see and touch. In *The Nature and Art of Workmanship*, he says: 'The extreme paucity of names for surface qualities has quite probably had the effect of preventing any general understanding that they exist as a complete domain of aesthetic experience, a third estate in its own right.'

Pye tells us that what we want a surface to express is not the properties of a material but qualities. Properties, he says, are 'out there', and they are immutable; qualities are subjective and are in our heads. One can test this pretty quickly: warmth, friendliness, timelessness are not properties of a piece of old polished oak; they are qualities projected by us. (That there is a similar cause and effect relationship between many people and their emotional response to a piece of oak deserves a separate account.) The tensile strength or the liability to combustion of the piece of wood are properties. In fact, Pye's argument needs qualifying here: designers or engineers do go some way in expressing certain kinds of properties – a steel rod can be made to bow in such a way that it performs its task as a component in a construction and also, by doing what it does, expresses its tensile properties. Either way, the craftsman working a surface is in one sense an artist – he (or she) is leaving his subjective mark in how he decides to treat the surface.

A craftsman must also be a 'scientist' as well as an artist. And this returns us to Pye's own work as a craftsman. In order to produce the best surfaces and the best performances you have to know what your material is and what your material will do. You cannot act, as so many designers and architects act, as though you are above the world looking down on it, specifying what is ideal. See how detailed is Pye's knowledge of wood in this little extract from an article written for *Crafts* magazine in January 1981. In it he remarked how far so many people's knowledge of surface has atrophied through their reliance on photographs rather than empirical scrutiny of the thing itself. He then goes on to discuss preparing a wood surface for polishing: 'All hardwoods contain sap vessels or pores which are hollow pipes running lengthways up the tree. If a cylinder with its grain parallel to the lathe's axis is turned smooth, these pores are exposed all over it and appear as very small and usually short troughs or gutters. Now if a scraper lying horizontal on the T–rest is used on the cylinder, its edge, being parallel with most of the troughs, catches in each one as it comes past and tears microscopic splinters off the upper edge of it.'

## An overview

David Pye's work contains elements of the designer and the craftsman. His bowls and boxes are easy to understand forms and they present none of the complexities that some kinds of contemporary art present to the understanding. He represents design rather than art in craft.

For, broadly speaking, the contemporary craft world divides between those people who are making objects that can be used, or look as if they can be used, and those who produce objects that are plainly useless and have ambitions to be taken seriously as art objects. This distinction is rather crude because even function can be compromised.

For example, fans of handicraft can enjoy the experience of faulty function. A famous American potter, Betty Woodman, produced some beautiful scalloped, large cups. A delight to clasp in both hands, the cups were popular but hopelessly unstable in their saucers. It never mattered. One owner remarked that the fault made him more careful; it obliged him to pause and think about drinking the tea, making it a little ritual. It is important to recognize, however, that although a lot of craft work has function much further down the list of priorities than would be acceptable in design, there remains for a number of potters, weavers and furniture makers the idea that good service to the client rests in the object being able to perform well.

The crafts world divides between those who have a conservative ideology, of whom Pye is a good example, and those who seek a form of decorative arts *avant garde* based often on a denial not only of function but also the primacy of skills. Certainly, in the 1980s we have seen a considerable growth in the category of unusable craft – a proliferation of objects that are inclined towards painting or sculpture.

In a sense, although they would loathe the idea, Bernard Leach and Michael Cardew are the fathers of the upswell in art-craft objects. For, as soon as people were willing to buy handmade pots because they liked their look rather than because they were cheap and useful, a trend begun whereby craft objects could be sold for their aesthetic content alone. And once the process had begun it was (and still is) unclear where you should stop. Once function has been set aside as a controlling criterion, the craftsperson runs into a peculiar area of no rules: if a thing has no longer to contain soup or be sat on or to keep someone warm, then it might as well take any form that is fancied.

Look, for example, at the United States. There exists in the United States some of the finest craftsmanship in the world – the traditional or, as one should say, the *quasi*-traditional craftsman in America is often awesome. At the same time there is a large and growing industry in art-craft, much of it abstract or non-figurative and all of it non-functional. The development of this phenomenon in the United States is not surprising because it is rooted in that peculiarly American invention – Abstract Expressionism.[1]

Obviously the craftsperson, especially the art-school trained craftsperson, was bound to be fascinated by developments in this kind of painting – even more so than with more formal, European abstract

*Few materials are malleable like clay; few allow the maker to leave the immediacy of the gesture of the moment frozen in three dimensions. This example of gestural ceramic form is by Irene Vonck (Holland).*

painting of the 1920s and 1930s – because of the presence of gesture, the mark of the hand and the arm. The mark of the hand is a very important element in the twentieth-century crafts, as will be discussed below. When craftsmen looked at modern painting they recognized that painting was no longer fulfilling any particular function other than simply to be there. When they reflected on the role of craft work, they recognized that, once the function of a craft work was taken away, what remained was – a thing: a 'thing' in the same sense that a Jackson Pollock is 'a thing', and for all intents and purposes without much content.

Moreover, as the craftsperson saw, what gave a Pollock or a Kline its content was gesture and 'expressiveness' – naturally, obviously, the craftsperson thought: 'I can do that.' Expressionism gave way to various kinds of other abstractions – formalisms in which shape and texture and colour and line were the prime considerations: really very much like flower arranging. Inevitably, many people in the crafts disciplines followed suit. For example, the Dutch ceramicist Irene Vonck makes vessel-like objects from sausages of clay. It is not a greatly skilled activity, although often the results are, to my taste, extremely attractive. In their rough, spontaneous fashion they are a pastiche. For, when you first glance at them you think they are richly embellished with modelling. Take a second look and you see the rough, scalloped trough where her hands have pulled and dug at the damp clay.

## Freedom from trade

The late 20th century offers the craftsperson a special economic environment to work in. The handicrafts of potting or weaving or woodworking in the late 20th century are practised under conditions unlike those of previous centuries. Handmade potting, weaving and the rest have stopped being trades as such and have changed class – changed from being working-class or artisan, commercial occupations into middle-class, creative, *art-like* activities. Art-like in the sense that the objects produced are made and bought primarily for contemplation. Moreover, the physical and moral pain which, it seems, is, if only to a degree, part of the operation of trade in the past has been exchanged for creative freedom.

Freedom from pain is one of the hallmarks of modern civilized society; it makes so much more creativity possible and it is the foundation of pleasure. What Elaine Scarry has to say in *The Body in Pain* about the nature of pain in work is of relevance to the way we view the work of the craftsperson (see also Chapter Four, pp. 88–90).

Scarry argues that intense pain, as achieved in torture, is world destroying: as the pain you are suffering increases, so your capacity to think about anything else is obliterated. She says: 'The ceaseless, self-announcing signal of the body in pain, at once so empty and undifferentiated and so full of blaring adversity, contains not only the feeling "my body hurts" but the feeling "my body hurts me".'

Repetitive pain of the kind induced by certain kinds of work or disease certainly reduces your world by presenting a barrier between you and the world and by constantly turning your body in on itself, ever threatening to negate for you the wider world of ideas and pleasures beyond.

Work, too, is a kind of pain. There are different kinds of painful labour. At its worst, at the closest it gets to actual torture, there is the work described by Karl Marx in *Capital*,[2] as in the case of a brickmaker, a woman, whose routine he documents. She was twenty-four years old and each day made two thousand bricks. She was assisted by two children who, in repeated trips throughout the course of the day, carried ten tons of clay up 30 feet of the wet sides of the clay pit and then for a distance of 210 feet. That was agony.

The industrialization of work probably made some work less painful but, as we know, it was and is a burden for many people. Simone Weil, the French philosopher and Christian, spent time working in factories in the 1930s. In an appeal to factory workers producing components of stoves, she wrote: 'Say if the work makes you suffer. Say if there are times when you can't bear it; if there are times when the monotony of the work sickens you; if you hate being always driven by the need to work fast; if you hate being always at the orders of the overseers.'

Even in creative work, pleasure depends upon the conditions under which it is done. In *The Nature and Art of Workmanship* David Pye recalls a conversation with an old wood turner. Pye notes that the wood turner used to make carved wooden spoons to be sold at fairs for tuppence apiece. 'At that price there was just time, when the spoon was finished, to look once at the inside, once at the outside, throw it over your shoulder on to the heap and start another.' Pye doubts if there could have been much pleasure in such work even though the spoons were, no doubt, a pleasure to look at.

When we read Pye's own description of his own work (as in the instance earlier in this chapter), however, we read of a man engaged in his work, enjoying the minute labour of it. It is a pleasure to read the description because the work described is free from stress, save that of having to concentrate, as one must in all workmanship of risk.

When a work process becomes commercially redundant it attracts new interest from those for whom commerce is not important. In the 1920s in Europe there was a deepening of interest in hand-weaving, hand-dyeing and hand-throwing. This interest, by the non-tradespeople of the middle classes, occurred at the point when the skills were nearly lost and when everyday manufacturing of cloth or pots had been taken over by mechanical methods.

In his autobiography *A Pioneer Potter* (published posthumously in 1988), Michael Cardew explains that when he took over the Winchcombe pottery in England in 1926 it was still possible to make the basic lines, such as washing pans and large flower pots, pay. But Cardew was in competition with commerce and the washing pans became less popular, presumably because the factories could supply enamelled metal pans more cheaply (and these would have had advantages over the ceramic ones by being lighter and more resilient). As for the large flower pots, he found that these too could not be produced competitively – factories made them cheaper. But Cardew found that a halfway-house product – halfway between trade and art – was practical. This product was a decorated range of useful pots and for a time he did a good trade in them – no one else was competing to undercut him.

Cardew, however, had not left Oxford University and given up the academic or musical life (he was passionate for Mozart) to become a trade potter. He was not in the pottery business *per se* – had he been, then he would have set about industrializing his processes. What he wanted to make (despite there being no *trade* demand for them) was big earthenware jars, the now famous cider flagons. He went ahead, made some and eventually he exhibited twelve of the best, gave them each (for him) vastly inflated prices, and put them in the annual exhibition of the then newly formed National Society of Painters, Sculptors, Engravers and Potters (1931). Most of them sold in the first day. Triumph. And, of course, release.

The release was from the economic constraints of trade competition. Objects that are sold on aesthetic grounds are not subject to competition by price. This fact alone has consequences for the nature of the work process. The removal of your product from the world of price competition takes you out of the awful treadmill that David Pye illustrated with his account of the spoon carver. It also builds in more freedom, more autonomy into the work process, thereby releasing some of the pain. If you can sell a few things on their intrinsic merit, irrespective of what other producers are making, then you can afford the time to make the product you want on your own terms. But in trade competition the competitive economy is like a machine and it, not you, dictates the terms.

Hence the phenomenon whereby a work process only becomes of interest to a middle-class practitioner when the trade element has dropped out – where trade and the economic constraints of price competitiveness and manufacturing efficiency are paramount, then scope for autonomy, choice and creativity in the work process is greatly diminished.

We can summarize the position as follows:

Contemporary craft is necessarily peripheral to all mainstream economic activity. If it comes too close to trade, then both the nature of the craftsperson's work and the nature of the artefact is compromised by the need to be price competitive with trade.

The activity of making craft today is quite different from when that craft was a trade. Today craft is produced out of a middle-class choice, as an expression of free will for an audience that has sufficient money – and perception – to afford useless objects of contemplation. What distinguishes craft from trade is a diminution in the amount of pain involved and a very considerable rise in the quotient of pleasure and self-fulfilment.

There is another factor. Many craftspeople earn a part or a very small part of their living from craft work, even though that craft work may fill up the most important part of their lives. They are supported by spouses or teaching. Some do make a full-time living, especially where the economy is strong enough to provide enough customers with surplus income and where, as in the cities of New York, Chicago and Los Angeles, for example, there are dealers and galleries interested in constructing a market for crafts that is analogous to that of the art market.

## Self-fulfilment

Setting to one side the area of art–craft, the *avant garde* movement that is sometimes anti-skill and anti-function, it is important to explore more fully the creative and other pleasures offered by crafts in their conservative mode. By conservative, I mean that recognizable, familiar

*One of our greatest pleasures is to be thoroughly involved in – and thus distracted by – our work. Engagement is a central goal for the modern craftsman. Shown here is Jim Patterson at his paper mill in Watchet, Somerset, UK.*

forms are to the fore; there is a premium on skill; and there is a conscious desire to serve a client as well as to make a creative 'statement'.

What attracts men and women to a craft is the promise it offers of 'work as a pleasurable end in itself'. These are activities that one willingly engages in for the pleasure of having one's full physical and mental attention absorbed. To 'lose oneself' in work is to enter a kind of active oblivion. All other ambitions, other than being watchful over the execution and development of the work, are temporarily banished.

Craftspeople are frequently awed by the image of creative autonomous work. In the search for ideals and idols of creative labour the
modern European and North American craftsperson has sought out
potential heroes – especially in Japan. In ceramics the contemporary
masters, such as the Japanese potter Shoji Hamada, have attracted
adulation, especially amongst Americans, not only for what they
produce but for the way in which they labour. And, of course, the way
in which potters such as Hamada work is the very antithesis of the
painful labour of a factory – including (and especially) the pain of
organized labour in Japanese car factories, for example. An idealizing
book about Hamada called *A Potter's Way and Work* by Susan Peterson
makes it clear that it is the work as well as the pots that we are to admire
(and understandably so). Hamada has great freedom in his work – he has
the time to choose what to make and when to make it and how fast to
make it (unlike Pye's wooden spoon carver). Hamada is much given to
aphoristic comments such as: 'These are the best pots, if they can be done
at the best times'; or 'Making a tea bowl means not thinking of making a
tea bowl.'

And here Susan Peterson describes Hamada making some pots: 'He
twirls the wheel with his stick and gets six revolutions before it slows
down. The cone of clay comes up irregularly, but he wants that, and he
opens a shape at the top of the hump with his left hand. As the tea bowl
bells out, he tends to throw it a bit off, raising an uneven spiral. Now and
then he puts a flat palm and two fingers on the left side of the clay,
pushing gently, throwing the bowl off centre, making a wobble or
causing an unevenness at the top. Hamada jokes with the boy and talks
for the visitors, explaining how he uses his hands. When they leave, he is
quieter and speaks in a different tone about his friend Kanjiro Kawai and
the poetry he wrote, and about the things they used to do together. The
bowls just seem to come up from the clay anyway, without thinking,
which is how he says they should come.'

To an extent this almost mystical approach to making can be
exaggerated: it appeals to Westerners and ought to be taken with a pinch
of scepticism. Nevertheless, it bears out a picture of self-fulfilment that
does seem idealistic provided we read a little between the lines –
Hamada had quite a support system from apprentices and family,
especially his wife. Being Japanese, he could count on the subservience
of the women around him.

The appeal of the Hamada retreat into the self-sufficient universe of his own self-directed work can be understood. One of the characteristics of contemporary culture is its demand that the individual constantly questions self and society. This questioning is a good thing; indeed, it is a necessary tool of cultural survival (see p. 104). But no individual, no culture can subject his or institutions to too much questioning; there has to be a belief in the innate values of an activity if the activity is to be pursued with any seriousness.

The best activities in the world are – obviously – the ones we love. Within these there will be work that is non-creative, yet it is possible to love non-creative work; and that is an important aspect of craft work.

In his autobiography, Michael Cardew discusses the routine exertion of kneading and preparing the clay prior to throwing on the wheel. He writes: 'I soon discovered that if you did it with the right rhythm and tempo, using the weight of your body rather than the muscles of your arm, you could knead for a long time without becoming tired . . . I found it to be one of those seemingly mindless or automatic hand processes which give a craftsman an unforseen bonus.' The concept of pleasurable labour, whether of a mechanical or of an overtly creative kind, is one to which all classes of workers aspire, but one which the working or mechanical classes seldom achieve because pleasure in work, as in much else, depends (usually) on freedom of choice.

What makes the menial task of pugging or kneading the clay a pleasure for Cardew is a combination of intelligence, skill and, above all, freedom of choice. What counts is the fact that he *wanted* to make pots, not that he was *obliged* to make them. The preparation of the clay was not a moral burden for him, since he was asking himself to do this task: no one was requiring it of him.

Studio handicrafts are not normally the result of a division of labour: the pleasure for the contemporary handicraftsperson is to do the whole production process personally because in so doing he or she is opposing and cutting free from a method of work that places the factory or the institution above the individual. The modern potter, who in Europe is almost bound to be middle class, secures his or her philosophical and practical freedom by retaining power over the whole process. Some potters go so far as digging their own clay. Few, however, can carry independence through entirely: you would have to be an extremist to seek to make the gas or the electricity that powers the kiln, or labour away grinding up the minerals (which you will have mined yourself) in order to produce glazes. The truth is that any manufacturing culture demands some co-operative labour and division of skills.

It is simply a measure of the modern craftsperson's economic freedom that he can choose to do more rather than less of the work because it pleases him so to do.

The crafts are a clear instance of an institution in which, as Baudrillard has said, 'the ideology of competition gives way to a philosophy of self-fulfilment'.[3]

However, in conservative crafts, of the kind practised by Pye, the fulfilment of *self* is a public as well as a private activity. Fulfilment comes from doing work that others can judge, using criteria that are generally accepted and shared. Shared criteria help to reduce the risk of arbitrary decision-making in one's own work. Shared criteria are the basis of skill.

Skill in art or craft communicates in at least two ways: as a means for making the concept or the metaphor of the work clearer, and as a 'thing' to be admired in its own right. If, for example, one adopts a craft such as hand throwing pots on the wheel – making cups or mugs or jars or bowls – then one is making things that fall into a tradition. This tradition is rich and diverse in the cultures that have contributed to it. Moreover, the traditions provide clear criteria by which contemporary work may be judged.

Thus when we say that this is a better bowl than that, we are able to agree on what it is we are making an assessment about: maybe the bowl sags somewhat rather than rising swiftly, maybe the proportion of the base to the rim feels and looks unbalanced. Or, if we have a lidded jar, we might argue that the lid does not fit well, that the handle is unpleasant to hold, or that the whole jar is too heavy in relation to its size. In looking at decoration we can make assessments about how well a decorative motif is drawn. We can have all sorts of discussion about the nature and criteria involved in decoration. For amateurs to know what the criteria are, what the 'rules' are within which they are operating, is reassuring and productive of good work. Craft activity of this kind offers a clear structure, agreed aims, common goals.

Shared criteria are the basis of skill and although only a few people may possess the intelligence and dexterity to perform well in carving or throwing at a wheel, many more people can share in the achievement by taking pleasure in it. The pleasure we are taking might be quite profound. What excites me about the small carved box described at the beginning of this chapter is its demonstration of integrity – a demonstration of a man who loves his work, who takes it as seriously as he can. We get a sense of knowing someone through their work. The American essayist Vicki Hearne, in her book *Adam's Task* (1986), says: 'Normally, our sense of whether or not someone knows something has partially to do with our sense of interest in and love for their subject – which is part of intelligence and integrity both. We prefer to have a mechanic who loves cars working on our engines. . . . '

If we make something for someone else to like and understand, then the criteria for success cease to be arbitrary and become communal. We are required to use our moral and aesthetic imagination by asking such questions as: will this chair be comfortable? Is it durable? Is it easy to move? What does it feel like to hold? Does its decoration make sense? Is the decoration there to delight or to cheat by disguising poor design or, worse, bad workmanship?

It would be misleading if, in describing the crafts as a middle-class activity, the impression is conveyed that they are elitist. To begin with, the 'middle classes' are the majority in Europe and the USA. Moreover, one of the very great attractions of crafts work is that it can be pursued to very high standards as a part–time, amateur activity.

What gives the crafts a potency is the participatory nature of their activity; it makes little sense to speak of an amateur industrial designer. David Pye calls the category of amateur I have in mind a 'part–time professional', but we are talking about the same animal. In Pye's *The Nature and Art of Workmanship* he writes: 'It is still commonly believed that a man cannot really learn a job thoroughly unless he depends on it for his living from the first and gets long experience at it. It is untrue. Two minutes experience teach an eager man more than two weeks teach an indifferent one. A man's earning hours and his creative hours can be kept separate and it may be that they are better separated.' Pye himself is an *amateur*; he has earned his living as a teacher and writer – in his spare time, he has carved wooden bowls.

One of the characteristics of a magazine such as the American journal *Fine Woodworking* is the amount of common agreement, shared purpose and indeed structure that the readers (many of them amateurs) share – the magazine encourages contributions from its amateur as well as its professional readership (such encouragement would never occur in a fine art magazine of equivalent status). Crafts activity in this area is not questioning or sceptical. It is intelligent but operating within a framework of agreed rules.

There is an important difference between the hobbyist and the amateur. The amateur does not earn his or her living from the work — but he or she might still, in most cases generally will, want to sell on to a consumer. The hobbyist might simply make things for the hell of it and not need to be especially self-demanding.

## The style of handicrafts

But what is it in the style of contemporary conservative crafts artefacts that makes the objects wanted by consumers whose desires and wants are catered for so cleverly and expertly by industry?

The Mexican writer Octavio Paz, in his essay 'Seeing and Using: Art and Craftsmanship' (*Convergences*, 1987), is interesting here. He says: 'The industrial object tends to disappear as a form and become one with its function . . . The industrial object forbids the superfluous; the work of craftsmanship delights in embellishments. Its predilection for decoration violates the principle of usefulness.'[4] Paz is not strictly accurate. Design and industry have moved on — as we have seen, the coupling of computer-driven machinery has brought in superfluous decoration once more although, in fairness to Paz, this decoration never intentionally interferes with the smooth function of the product. In many handmade products embellishment can add a quirkiness to function — this is especially true of the rich variety of non-ergonomic handles to be found on craft-produced pottery and glasswares.

But certainly Paz's insight that the industrial object disappears into its function is a vital one. It is this 'disappearance' that the craft-designer-maker (the difficulties in finding an adequate terminology persist) actively resists. Thus the handicrafts of the 20th-century arts and crafts movements oppose rather than serve or enhance industrial design.

The metaphorical content of handicraft rests in its expression of a way of labour and a way of life that is rare in modern manufacturing and rare in Western or Western-style economies. Quite often in this century 'modern' craftspersons have found it useful to exaggerate certain iconoclastic features of their craft as a form of product differentiation. A

*A hand-built cup and saucer by the Yugoslav ceramicist, Ljerka Njers, demonstrating a role for handcrafted domestic ware — the role is in the supply of the individualistic and the idiosyncratic. At the same time, this work does not subvert traditional decorative values but enhances and builds upon them.*

*(Opposite) This market scene from Philadelphia is another aspect of the anti-industrial aesthetic espoused by crafts — here demonstrated in retailing.*

wobbly line here, a slightly askew handle there, reminds the consumer that this thing is a product of the hand.

In contemporary manufacturing and consumerist societies it is relatively easy to be iconoclastic in style: any departure from the median standard of more or less flawless industrial production will either appear odd or special. Surface perfection is a sign of an industrial culture: in factories, whether they are producing automobiles or candy bars, a thing will be rejected by the quality–control department if there is a surface flaw, irrespective of whether or not it affects the performance, durability or taste of a product.

Flaws are barely tolerated in 'below the line' design and their presence is intolerable when they threaten the safety or efficient running of a machine. And in all those artefacts upon which we depend for our health, safety or our lives we can see that the styling and the finish avoids all hint of imperfection. The styling of transport, medical, industrial and domestic appliances suggests smoothness, efficiency and *order*. And it is only in the context of the *smoothness* of our society — smooth surfaces, smooth running, smoothly safe and smoothly reassuring industrial design — that the luxury of imperfection can be indulged.

Hand-produced ceramics and glass have, in particular, made a virtue of 'imperfection'. Here, for example, we see a vase by Lucie Rie which is a celebration of imperfection; a cup and saucer from Rosenthal, the West German factory, which is an excellent example of good, perfect and flawlessly predictable design; and, finally, a virtuoso but clearly handbuilt display, full of narrative content, by the American potter, Frank Fleming.

The Rosenthal is the median standard and its existence allows the likes of Rie to survive and do well — if we had yet to achieve Rosenthal's flawlessness, then Rie's pockmarks would be unwanted. We can relish

(Above) *Marcello Morandini's teaset (Italy), designed for Rosenthal (West Germany).*

(Opposite) *The American potter Frank Fleming continues, via handbuilding, his country's insatiable need for narrative art in its artefacts.*

(Right) *Lucie Rie's vase (Austria/UK) succeeds in its roughness because in the late twentieth century we have succeeded in securing the smooth in the general run of our consumer lives.*

her 'imperfections' knowing that an alternative is always possible. The demand for craft, like the demand for 'design', is based on a wish to differentiate oneself from the general impulses of society while at the same time knowing that one belongs. Thus, if everyone has a cupboard full of the good and acceptable industrial wares, the studio crafts offer a comforting extra: a thickening to the domestic aesthetic or, if you like, a foil.

There is also another category of craft in which the objects demonstrate a formidable virtuoso and intricate perfection – objects that display so much redundant perfection that we know they had to be handmade and that that such handmaking was either carried out in spite of the economic imperative or because someone very rich was willing to patronize it. This is to be found in some jewelry and some wood- and metalwork.

In fact, one of the interesting outcomes of the competitiveness between the handicrafts and industrial manufacture is that in some areas of contemporary handicraft – wood furniture, for example – we are seeing virtuoso performances unrivalled by craftsmen of previous centuries. Contemporary wood craftsmen have decided to compete with the machined certainties of industry by making ever more cunning elaborations – beautifully perfect simple joints are no longer enough to distinguish the modern machine from the craftsman's hand because such joints are merely the day-to-day routine of automatic routers. In particular, there are American craftsmen making furniture by hand who have scaled great heights in technical skill because they have been chased like cats up trees by the doggedness of industrial performance. Consequently, they have developed styles that deliberately reveal complicated or subtle joints, or which demand carving, bending or twisting the wood into organic forms of baffling surface geometries. Many of the contemporary major figures in woodsmanship are American, among them Wendell Castle and Sam Maloof.

'Perfect' and 'imperfect' are comparative terms. Not all that is both 'unsmooth' and handmade is imperfect: the craft of weaving baskets from willow, for example, has had a successful revival in the United States and in Britain – and there is a 'rough' perfection in the construction of such things which is more than skin deep. A handmade basket is one of those examples whose style, surface beauty and 'below the line' design and manufacture are all at one with sound function and durability. The

*Baskets, like unembellished iron bridges, lay bare the logic of their existence. Very few industrially produced artefacts do likewise. This example is by David Drew, UK.*

handmade basket, such as that by David Drew illustrated above, is only imperfect in the cost of its labour.

As well as being comparative terms, 'perfect' and 'imperfect' are also culturally specific – for example, the kind of ceramics used by the Japanese in their tea ceremonies are regarded as beautiful by the Japanese even though to many Western eyes the pots appear misshapen and crude.

## An aesthetic in opposition?

What does the crafts world in Europe and the USA amount to? It is one of those loose-fit 'institutions', affordable by wealthy societies with mature cultures, that offer a haven for the many people who, one way or another, are in opposition to or at least uncomfortable with their society. There is nothing automatically subversive about this opposition, nor is it often a wholesale rejection of society. What the phenomenon of the contemporary crafts world offers people is a little more space to organize themselves the way they want to. At the most basic level of craft as a hobby we can see that the crafts offer the conformist and conservative individual an opportunity to construct his or her own world in the time that is left over from serving society as a clerk or a teacher or a telephone engineer or whatever. Other men and women have gone further and by setting up a crafts workshop they attempt, sometimes successfully, to live all their time to a pattern and order that they themselves determine and regulate.

It is probable that other people, equally intelligent and creative, envy the craftspeople but for a variety of dutiful and practical reasons plough careers that are danced to the rhythms that others set. And it is these intelligent but conformist salary 'slaves' who make up the constituency that buys the work peddled by the contemporary craftspeople. For what is wanted by the conformists and supplied by so many craftspeople is a lively craft aesthetic that is dressed in familiar forms: pottery that looks handmade, has a lively bearing and texture but is quasi-traditional in form; likewise furniture; likewise textiles.

In its own way this work is part of the craft aesthetic in opposition. It opposes and it is different to what Main Street and technology has to offer. Main Street and technology can offer perfection; the crafts can offer you warm fallibility or friendly flaws. (Because contemporary craftware has no function and therefore fulfils no responsibilities, it does not matter if there are design or construction faults.) The aim of much craft is not workaday perfection because we can buy that elsewhere: the aim is more to do with putting people back into communication with one another. Complex virtuosity is another matter. The virtuosity of the handmade also communicates, person to person. It is the in-between world of technology that is mute. There is something special about the notion of someone making a thing particularly for you. There is also something important psychologically in seeing the mark of the hand of the maker in a work. Technology is efficient, but it is deeply anonymous.

The backward-looking nature of the majority of crafts is an essential feature of its economic success. If technology had developed in a different guise – wearing the textures and forms of a lumpen, organic, richly textured aesthetic, for example – then the crafts world would have had to respond with finesse and a 'machine' look.

It would be inaccurate, however, to imply a total fracture between crafts and industrial design. They are in opposition but not at all points.

There is a sense in fact in which handicraft forms have had an influence on mainstream design – an influence that is potent in Scandinavia and waxes and wanes and waxes again in the USA. A brief review of 20th-century design in Scandinavia will show that in design for the home – ceramics, glassware, tableware, furniture and soft furnishings – the language of the design is very close to that of handicrafts. Even where things are machined they retain a 'handmade' look. Bearing in mind that the Scandinavian countries have had largely social democratic governments for the last fifty years and have maintained a policy of social welfare and creating the ideal middle-class state, and taking into account the metaphor of conservative crafts being warm, humane, comforting, it is not surprising that the craft aesthetic has remained dominant.

Even more to the point, the influence of Scandinavian design – with its emphasis upon the idea of the vessel, of the enclosing form – has been consistently popular (since the 1920s) in the United States. The apotheosis of the craft/vessel/Scandinavian design influence upon American design was reached in forms for furniture by designers such as Charles Eames and Eero Saarinen in the 1940s and early 1950s. These designs have remained influential to this day; indeed, the organic shape, the vessel and the womb are still potent metaphors in contemporary American design and there is little doubt that the 1990s will see a revival or re-interpretation of the Eames look.

There remains, especially in the USA, West Germany, the Netherlands and Britain, a sub-theme in the crafts story. There has been an opposition by some craftspeople to the main crafts ethos of serving the home with familiar forms: a significant number of craftspeople have rejected *conservative* values and *conservative* crafts. Hence there has been an anti-skill movement and, above all, an anti-craft as consumer product movement.

In Britain and West Germany and the Netherlands men like Ron Arad (Israel/UK) and groups like *Hard Werken* (Netherlands) have indicated that the ideas are often more important than the objects. In England especially, there was a strong movement in the 1970s to throw skill out of the window. Most of the younger generation of English art-school trained graduates cannot draw or model or throw or make things very well. One of the reasons for the (temporary) downgrading of skill as an important ingredient in craft is connected with political attitude. If most craft was bought by the bourgeoisie it was because they found that the crafts gave them solace.

A significant body of craftsmen and craftswomen did not, in the 1970s and 1980s, want to give comfort to their clients; they would rather disturb them. Younger craftsmen dumped skill because skill was a bourgeois hang-up and in any case it was easier not to bother. The same young makers also subverted familiar forms.

From the conservative viewpoint the subversion of skill is resented. The other side to the argument is that the vocabulary available to the contemporary craftsman has expanded. There exists now in the West (especially in countries such as England and America where the old industries have suddenly become history) a lot of 'old' material that has fallen out of the technological world. This old-fashioned 20th-century industrial 'junk' that was, thirty years ago, still competitive technology, is now available for reworking into the crafts as part of an aesthetic of opposition to the current technology. Thus early electrical equipment and early machine parts are now being worked into craft objects by young artist craftspeople.

Nostalgia, such an important ingredient in craft, has moved on. It is also arguable that the craftspeople who have adopted such assemblage techniques of the 1980s were repeating the strategy of some of the early 'machine age' artists such as Marcel Duchamp – fascinated by the beauty of late Victorian machinery and kitchen gadgetry, as he demonstrated with his retrieval of the metal bottle rack in 1914.

The imagery and artefacts of the smokestack industries are now as rich in potential *craft* meaning as old potteries and basket-weaving workshops. The youngsters have been radical by sifting through the urban scrapheaps for anti-bourgeois imagery and in essence they have helped the crafts world catch up with modern history. Crafts have, in one sense, simply caught up with the pace of change. The crafts world is a reactive institution – it reacts to changes and trends, and it seeks to offer an alternative vision and range of metaphors.

Yet, in the complexity of contemporary crafts there are other extremes: the making of unique objects that are so ostentatiously lavish in the time spent making them that they are intended to acquire the sort of rich person 'art' status of the Fabergé egg syndrome.

In America sometime sculptors like Wendell Castle have tuned successfully to furniture-making and then, as they have developed, started to reach for art status by producing furniture that is ostentatious, even fabulous in its craftsmanship and materials, as though it were commissioned by a self-indulgent monarch. Castle, however, has not gone as far down the road of faddishness as other, less able American furniture designer–makers for whom post-modernism has been a great source of delight.

It is ironic that whereas among applied artists, architects and designers post-modernism has meant an optimistic splurge, a succession of across-the-border raids into history to steal the baubles of past styles, amongst literary academics the post-modernist debate has generated views bordering on nihilism. Post-modern excesses in American crafts have built up to a rainbow motley: coloured balls, pyramids, touches of Egyptian and/or Roman detailing and other gratuitous decoration have been pressed into service to turn handmade objects into quasi-sculptures.

In the end, and perhaps pessimistically, the late twentieth century finds artists, designers, craftspeople and perhaps the majority of us faced with a disquieting piece of knowlege. We are excluded from the real *avant garde*, or cutting edge, of contemporary culture; we are all marginalized. The heart of the contemporary *avant garde* in the West is not craft or art or the modernism versus post-modernist debate – the heart is theoretical physics and applied technology. How many of us are able to enter the conceptual landscape of the new physics or are at home in the craft of computer software construction?

Yet this is not quite all. For if we are marginal to the main thrust of contemporary culture – excluded not by lack of talent but by complete ignorance – then we are free to find interest and diversion where we may. Hence the continued success of twentieth-century crafts.

# 7

# DESIGN FUTURES

# Conservation and Conservatism

In the 1990s more designers and manufacturers will discover what some have already affirmed: that money is to be made – and virtue gained – from environmental issues. Politicians are appearing greener, and the concept of holistic design that takes into account all the consequences of manufacturing, from raw materials to the disposing of the object once it is discarded, will by the end of the 1990s form a greater part of the design and business orthodoxy. The principles of such practice will feature in the teaching provided on the various courses of art, design, technology and business. Designers may even get into the habit of asking themselves (without the prompting of lobbyists) what impact their work will have on the world.

There is no chance that, in the West, the approach to holistic, environmentally sensitive design will be puritan; you cannot make a lot of money from hair shirts. What will happen, what *is* happening, is clear: as a part of people's growing affluence and desire for variety and quality of life, they want diversity in nature to be maintained, and they want to be healthier.

To an extent the demand for conservation and greening is a natural consequence of the consumer phenomenon of the post-Second World War period. In Chapter Five, it was remarked that there is a new democracy in industrial design whereby technology is giving us things of a quality that even the rich cannot rival with their greater purchasing power. If the rich do have access to a better environment, however, the logic of the extension in quality in the domain of the not-so-rich makes the environment and its benefits the next area of consumer interest. More and more people are discontented with what has happened to the places where they have their foreign holidays, to where they leisure at weekends, to the quality of their street. Having filled the home and the garage, they direct their eyes outwards. Envy and a refusal to be put upon are as useful ingredients in the greening of the world as they have been in the browning of it.

The hegemony of the advertiser, which both thrills and appals post-modernist theorists, will be in a partial retreat, not through self-discipline, not through law, but through the continued efforts of lobbyists and single-issue groups who, provided the media remain relatively free, will put their case and influence consumers. This, in turn, will influence retailers and they will make their demands on suppliers.

Growing consciousness of the world as an object in itself, which is to be regarded, cherished and looked after, is one example of positive thinking, and a rebuff to the modish pessimism and elitist ironic posing developed by some of the post-modernist theorists of the 1980s.

It is unlikely (and undesirable) that people's need for variety, for distraction and, of course, for employment will diminish. But it is possible, perhaps probable, that the *fashion* in design will be for things that are longer lasting and better quality. Already as I write post-modernism is deemed to have had its fashion – for the time being; a new version of modernism is being talked about – more stylish but with durability and excellent build-quality as part of the design and production specification. Much post-modernist design, especially in architecture, appears to be all too temporary and insubstantial. Insubstantiality is the wrong metaphor for a generation that is aware of the planet's vulnerability. With a growing agreement to conserve, protect and to make progress with care, we might realistically predict a style that expresses conservative rather than ironic values.

## Advertising and ideology

Much has been written about the power of the advertising industry. In *The Want Makers* (1988), Eric Clark describes systems for targeting goods at specific groups of people, among them ACORN (A Classification of Residential Neighbourhoods) and VALS (Values and Lifestyles). These systems identify who wants what and who can afford to buy it. As Clark says: 'It only works where the amount of material collected on people is vast to an almost unimaginable degree and where computers enable it to be sorted and used in countless different ways and combinations.' The fact is that this information and the means of handling it are available and are used in support of ACORN and similar classifications.

There are, we all know, various kinds of advertising; they cover a spectrum of sophistication and quality from mini, 45-second feature films to blunt 'here it is, come and get it' promotions. Compared with North-West Europe, television advertising in the USA is plain, short and centres on bargain prices. But, in its more sophisticated forms, an advertisement describes a whole world: it presents the service or the commodity to be sold in a situation in which every other item and person (or animal) has been most carefully selected, groomed, lit and cued. This is obvious to us on reflection, but important none the less because it is the total control of the mini-world presented in the advertisement that gives it an appeal which borders on poignancy, the poignancy of beauty seen but unattainable by you.

The craft of advertising is complex. True, the creators of advertisements are dealing with fictions, but these must strike chords with real people in the real world. Of course, Jean Baudrillard's 'hall of mirrors' thesis (p. 104) argues that increasingly we cannot tell the difference between who we are, and how we are presented by these fictions. But is this so? The experience is, surely, that we can tell the difference, and sometimes the difference hurts us.

Take, as an example, physical ugliness, which, as much as skin colour, moulds and directs lives in ways that people do not like to acknowledge. The old emollient, that 'It does not matter what you look like but what you are', is untrue. Ugliness repels people – repulsion is a part of the meaning of ugliness. Consequently, ugly people are shaped either by rejection or by the need to adopt strategies by which they can displace their physical unattractiveness with other means. They can, for example, seek to be *nicer* to people than average, or they can seek greater wealth than average (and hence buy favours).

Ugly people are unavoidably second class in modern, consumerist societies. Day by day in magazines, television and films they are reminded of what they don't and can never have – beauty. Material happiness revolves around beauty and the concomitant pleasures of the flesh. All other material effects are palliatives by comparison. Consumerism is based on selling these palliatives – and at the heart of consumerism there is the photograph.

Professional photography, a business pivoted on advertising, sells two commodities – beauty, plus the specific product advertised. Professional photography fuels pain through pleasure – the pain is in the impossibility of becoming beautiful, if one is ugly, the pleasure in seeing beauty (seeing beauty is *always* a pleasure). The pleasure is, of course, shot through with regret, even loss.

In his book *Beauty In History* (1988), Arthur Marwick explains that since the 1960s international travel, electronic information, satellite technology, an explosion of visual information and the marketing of youth have vastly increased our awareness of beauty and provided opportunities as never before to compare and contrast. Our sense of discrepancy, of flawed physical being, has been sharpened.

The photograph occupies an especially important place in consumerism: professional pictures of beauty set the standards, fix the commodity; you measure up or fail. In contradiction to Baudrillard, you are only too aware of the difference between the real and the unreal, or the real and the other aspect of the real.

None the less, distinguishing between how we are and how 'they' are in an advertisement is easy because we know the facts. We know how we live, how we look, how much money we have – and we are therefore aware how far away we are from fiction presented to us. But in a host of other ways we are in the advertiser's power unless we are active about it. For example, unless we know how a product is produced, we have no idea of the relative morality of the object or service being sold. A great many consumerables have a host of hidden truths: the contents of the kitchen – cleaning fluids, abrasives and polishes – are highly damaging to the environment both in their production and in their disposal (into the drains and sewers and eventually rivers and seas); they are also tested extensively on animals, causing very great pain. The same is true of many toiletries. None of this, obviously, intrudes on the advertisement. The advertising industry's function is to ensure that different and unpleasant realities are severed from pleasant ones.

Moreover, although graphic design is not a subject in this book, it is worth noting that graphic designers have played the role of the 'interface' between advertisement and reality. Their pretty packaging helps to pull some of the advertisement's gloss into the daily reality of the supermarket. The packaging is full of gambolling animals or healthy happy native workers or whatever else is designated to play a part in the disjunction of one reality from another.

But advertising, especially television advertising in Europe, is changing its emphases. It is more or less agreed in two of the world's three centres for advertising, New York and Tokyo, that the third, London, is a creative centre of the craft. One reason has been the extraordinary amount of money spent on television advertising by the British government, which has throughout the 1980s been selling off to the public the big service industries that were state owned. These industries, once they have been privatized, have tended to keep advertising as a part of a general exercise in promoting themselves. Other industries have followed suit. The advertisements sell not a single object, nor just a bundle of services, but an ideology. Imperial Chemicals Industries, British Petroleum and British Gas are busy showing themselves as having a modern world view combining humanism with technology. They are lavish productions and are the natural heirs to a cinematic tradition in Britain of soft, documentary propaganda dating from the Post Office Film Unit of the late 1930s.

The development of the ideological advertisement is of interest because it confirms an understanding that people, the public, the consumers, are, in fact, interested in values. How far we are willing to believe in the ideology of the caring, humane, world-conscious company is a moot point (vigilant scepticism is probably desirable). None the less, the growth in the late 1980s of a propaganda about values is of interest in an age which some writers have characterized as either value less or interested only in materialism.

## The real thing

The advertiser has the advantage over the product designer: the designer's objects have to perform; they can be tested and found wanting. Moreover, the consumer's expectations are upwardly mobile. The designer is always returned to the complaint, 'Why don't things work better than they do?'

In manufacturing there is less and less left to chance; and during the 1990s we can expect to see a growth in expert systems – computer-driven programmes in which strategies are worked out, tactics agreed, procedures codified and broken down into logical systems. Expert systems are applicable to almost any productive process, including education and medicine. Design can be included as well. As manufacturers and consumers become more demanding, the licence for designers to get it wrong will decrease. And so, just as general practitioners in medicine are discovering the benefits of possessing an expert system on their micro-computer to help them remember the vital questions that will help them achieve a correct diagnosis, so too the designer will relish some similar support. Hence it is appropriate to focus on the issue, broached in Chapter Four, of product semantics.

Klaus Krippendorf, Professor of Communications at the University of Pennsylvania, and Reinhart Butter, Professor of Industrial Design at Ohio State University, have – with their departments – worked on an exploration of the symbolic and ergonomic qualities of forms. In essence, product semantics explores the relationship between the designer, the object, the user, and the object/user and their environment. As Krippendorf and Butter say, 'The designer creates forms that report about themselves.' The core of their work is obvious, but obviousness is a part of the usefulness of expert systems and strategies because it is the obvious in design that tends to go wrong. For example:

- Making different kinds of objects look different. When they are too much alike, they can cause disaster. Examples include emergency equipment or the potentially critical situations of the locomotive driver's cab, aircraft, cockpit, operating theatre, or control room of a power station.
- Making an object safe to use. The hot/cold adjustment on shower units is a notorious area of danger – scalding water can kill. Other areas include making sure that the user knows which part of an object is designed for him/her to engage with, and which is not.
- Helping people to get the best out of an object; the software programs for micro-computers are mostly underused.
- Helping people to feel good.

Krippendorf and Butter say[1] that they are not in the business of styling; nor is their work about a new kind of psychological functionalism. We can ignore these protests. For whatever reason, product semantics practitioners are hung up about their own image and employ a language that is a pastiche of the scientific. But the faulty marketing of product semantics should not obscure the importance of the content.

The symbolic content of objects can become the most important aspect of a design even to the point where symbolism compromises use (but never safety). Of course, symbolism, aesthetics and taste blend into one, but it is surprising how many unsatisfactory objects are well liked despite their bad behaviour or outdatedness.

Some of the classic examples in this regard are in personal transport. Throughout the world there are people who prefer to drive the noisy, ugly, not very spacious and old-fashioned Volkswagen 'Beetle' whose provenance is in the late 1930s. In Britain there are still people willing to buy the Citroen 2CV, a slow, wobbly chicken-shack on wheels. In the USA, in spite of Japanese imitations that are much cheaper and technologically more developed, the Harley Davidson motorcycle reigns triumphant.

It is worth noting that in some classes of objects, especially things connected with work or with the kitchen, ugliness is a symbolic advantage. It works in one or all of several ways. In the example of the 'Beetle' or the 2CV it is a part of the aesthetics of resistance – the cars stand out from the crowd and, certainly in the case of the 2CV, it is a statement that the driver does not take driving and cars seriously or fetishistically. However, ugliness can, as discussed in Chapter Four in the example of the jug kettle (p. 98), speak of the transcendence of safety over chicness. Within limits, ugliness can also convey technological advance: it looks awful, but that's because it is so new you are not familiar with it.

Symbolism has an important role in the demystification of objects – and demystification is a popular way among younger designers in the late 1980s for providing themselves with a reason for existing (compare Chapters One (p.19) and Four (p. 98)). Certainly it is true that technology has raced ahead of the understanding of most of us; more than that, as discussed in Chapter Four (p. 84), so much technology is invisible. Invisibility is not necessarily synonymous with being difficult to understand, but unless we see how a thing moves, it is hard to comprehend its guts. For most of us the inside of the old-fashioned transistor radio is meaningless, except when you twiddle the tuning knob on the case and see the parts of the tuning condenser move. 'Tuning in' then has a visible meaning.

But we are hardly inconsolable about our loss of comprehension. On the whole, rather few of us care: the gains are so considerable in new technology and our intellects are so engaged on things other than worrying how electronic tools work – provided we can work them.

The micro-computer is one of the most interesting examples of a tool that is incomprehensible in its working and difficult to work. Now, being sensible and vigilant citizens, we do require reassurance about new technology, especially computer technology. We want the reassurance, for example, that the computer is not being used against us by 'them'. No amount of friendly hardware design or product semantics can compensate for the fear or suspicion that this or that machine is, in some way, malicious or treacherous. The possibility of the state or your bank using the computer against your best interests is a political and civil rights matter of fundamental importance – and beyond the competence of design to do anything about.

However, designers can do something about designing the means by which we can work the computer to its full potential. Very few micro-computers are used for more than word processing, but very few word-processing packages are used to their full capacity. Neither the hard- nor the software is designed for easy learning (although things have improved greatly via the innovations of the Apple Mackintosh).

The modern designer has a huge problem. He or she is faced with having to find forms and processes that enable individuals of unpredictable ability, attention span and tolerance to use systems which, in their naked reality, are extraordinarily complicated. The designer's task is not made easier by the fact that contemporary European and North American cultures have rapidly centred upon the view that everything, including learning, can be pain free. This is unfortunate because it is not often the case that all learning can be made simple or painless. None the less, we can expect both 'things' and 'processes' to be designed in such a way that entry into the first levels of use is easy, and that transition from one level of complexity to another is designed with logic and with the moral imagination that centres upon what the user is likely to have grasped. I use the term 'moral' deliberately because 'moral' involves the sympathetic and imaginative act of 'putting one's self' into the other person's shoes – it is the basis of teaching.

The designers' tasks are further complicated by the fact that consumer groups are composed of different generations who will have different levels of 'product literacy'. Today's teenagers are computer literate in most ways – they are at home with the textures, sounds and shapes of computers. Yet many older people, though they will have 'noticed' the equipment, will, none the less, have ignored it – it is still unfamiliar.

Older people may have different psychological and emotional needs to younger people; they may not welcome the visible manifestations of change. One can caricature this by imagining that some consumers might welcome the microwave oven, but prefer to see it dressed up as part of an old kitchen range. In any case, a lot of people, including children (especially young chidren), prefer order and stability to constant flux. We may all, as members of television- and video-saturated societies, have become used to very rapid changes in imagery and like the quicksilver quality of televisual images but, since we do appear to hold onto the distinction (Baudrillard notwithstanding) between the TV and our world, we seem also to prefer (and work very hard at) constancy and order.

## Design and society's roots

Whatever we or Reinhart Butter can say about an object's relationship with a consumer's emotions, intellect and imagination, it is also worth attending to design's relationship with the ideology of the culture that produces it. Indeed, it is the ideological relationship between the object and the consumer that lies behind the discussions about design and the rich in Chapter Five and craft versus design in Chapter Six.

In his essay 'What is at Stake in the Debate on Postmodernism?' (1987)[2] Warren Montag pointed out that although the overviews of contemporary society provided by the leading contributors to the debate were of great interest and importance, they were 'situated at such a great distance from the diverse objects they seek to describe that real specificities resolve into one blurred, harmonious totality.'

Among the specificities are those concerned with the institutions and frameworks which give meaning, structure, order and authority to our daily lives. It is one thing to be concerned about the mega-workings of capitalism *per se* or, at the other extreme, the vocabulary of form in an object (where do you put the switches?). The one viewpoint is too distant, the other too close. What generates the ideologies that provide the basis for meaning, the values in which all our work – design, science, art, manufacturing – are rooted?

Our roots are not in advertising or television; these twins do reflect the ideologies that bind us together but they do not generate values – they build on what already exists.

It might seem that the late 20th century is the age of scepticism; if this was true then Western society would be faced with a moral crisis. For, in its extreme form, scepticism undermines everything and everyone; it legitimises every act of cruelty, neglect and intolerance because it denies the point or purpose of anything. Values are destroyed if purpose is used as a yardstick. God used to provide a purpose, so did Marx. Today we are post-God (some of us), or post-Marx.

However, there is a profound difference between sceptical theory and human experience. In human lives there are a variety of experiences that are not dependent upon the notion of purpose. To ask what the point is of the love you feel for your child is, in practical moral terms, a meaningless question. The emotion of belief in or commitment to or involvement in those things which we can call 'ends in themselves' rebuff scepticism by rendering the sceptic's question itself pointless.

Some obvious ends in themselves include: interesting work, gardening, sport, companionship, listening to stories – and trying to find out how quarks work. Most, if not all the things which we take delight in as ends in themselves, depend upon the co-operation of other people or their agreement in our 'right' to pursue our interests. Our rights, however, are guaranteed by limitations and rules that are contained in our social institutions.

The contemporary philosopher who has best understood and articulated the importance of roots, and who has best explained the concept of the institution, is Roger Scruton, Professor of Aesthetics at Birbeck College, London. His book, *The Meaning of Conservatism* (1980), has a chapter called 'The Autonomous Institution' to which I am indebted.[3]

Scruton cites several examples of institutions such as competitive sport, the family, law and education. This is what he says about sport (and see also my comments about the crafts, pp. 153–159): 'The aim of a team is of course to win. But winning is defined by the rules of the game, and cannot be achieved except within the institution that defines it . . . Members of a team sometimes earn money; but the interest of football for those who are immersed in it lies in the game and its outcome . . . Football (or Ice Hockey, Baseball etc.) is also an institution. It is an arrangement which can outlive its individual members, and which offers them a transcendent bond of membership.'

Later on in the same chapter Scruton considers a much looser but still coherent example. 'Consider American rural society. It is neither barbarous, nor civilised, nor decadent. It is of no great interest to the outside world, but seems, despite that, to get on happily with itself. And we find in this society a proliferation of clubs and organizations, even old habits of craftsmanship that have disappeared from Europe. This is partly due to the lack of governmental presence. The American state is not given to regimenting its citizens into forms that are alien to them, and while the resulting chaos of childish eccentricities may have little appeal to an outsider, it is clear that it is not without considerable consoling power for those who engage in creating it.'

We gain our values and meaning through the variety of communal and corporate activities; we derive consolation and pleasure through the pursuit of ends in themselves. We celebrate our institutions and their values through ritual, through decoration, through their symbolic elaboration in artefacts and architecture. Our institutions are sources for symbolic meaning.

Good corporate designers understand implicitly the concept of the ideology of the institution. Corporate design, especially in its late 1980s manifestation, offers more to a company than a change of logo. Today, when a design company is commissioned to redesign a company's image the designers begin with an audit of the company's values. Staff and management are questioned about their work, morale, aims of the company, quality of internal communications and overall ethos. The intention is to report to the management on what the actual state of the company is, help it get closer to its ideals, and devise designs which will represent the ideals and ideology both internally to the employees, and externally to the public. General values include those of service, efficiency, reliability and courtesy.

Corporate identity design is not only about the internal audit and presentation of the company's ideals through design; it is also an acceptance of the fact that all institutions, including private, public and state-run companies, draw sustenance from the overriding social institutions of society, including the law. No doubt, there is a huge amount of hypocrisy with companies, like people, merely pretending to live up to the values they perceive other people expect. That, for our purposes, is beside the point.

The point for designers is, that, in an age of scepticism, more and more weight is being given by societies to the social rules, obligations and institutions that provide continuity and service in all its moral complexity. Never have so many people – whether described as citizens or consumers – been so well served, protected, cared for (that they are not served, protected or cared for sufficiently well is another argument; the point is that, on balance, there is some progress). Moreover, in the last years of this century we are seeing an emphasis upon pan-national social obligations, and these obligations, and the belief in the absolute values they contain, are reflected in such developments as the concern for environmental issues discussed above.

If we cast an eye back towards Charles Jencks' symbolic house (p. 106) we might say that the context, the institution he was using to give meaning to his design was too big – the whole of world civilization with substantial parts of the cosmos thrown in for good measure. But the instinct was right, and, in a sense, the need to define the present through symbolic references to the past is an ingredient that can contribute to the acceptability and humanitarian shaping of all design, especially that for the home.

One of the most important things designers can do is to symbolize continuity and reflect, both in the form and in the materials and processes used to shape the design, an understanding that the object has an impact upon the world. This is not to argue for nostalgia, nor to fly in the face of demands by fashion. It is, however, to argue for the importance of ensuring familiarity in design – and of employing the moral imagination.

Only such imagination guarantees that a design is of practical service and that the wider considerations, including environmental ones, are included in fulfilling the design objective.

What is cheering is that the moral commitment to wanting to change things for the better is as strong as ever. What is more, this commitment is tempered by the realization that all change should be careful and based, not on wishful thinking, but knowledge – especially knowledge through research and applied science of the consequences of our design upon our health, other species and the world at large.

# Notes on the text

## CHAPTER 2

1  Schama, Simon *The Embarrassment of Riches*, Collins, 1987.
2  Hayek, F.A. *The Road to Serfdom*, Ark, 1986, p. 27.
3  Hayek, F.A. *op cit.*
4  See Barnett, Correlli *The Audit of War*, Macmillan, 1986, for an examination of this in respect of British manufacturing industry.
5  McCoy, Esther 'The Rationalist Period', in *High Style* catalogue, Whitney Museum of American Art, New York/Martin Books, New York, 1985, p. 131. She says: 'Exactness was a necessity in the design of much of the material used in combat during the war and, as might be expected, the habit of using decimal tolerance carried over to peacetime design.'
6  Kennedy, Paul *The Rise and Fall of the Great Powers*, Unwin Hyman, 1988, p. 359. It is in its role as the 'world's policeman' that the USA has become seen as a threat to the integrity of other cultures. Japan, on the other hand, has steadfastly refrained from taking sides too often in foreign affairs, perhaps because it is bad for trade.
7  *Design Magazine*, June 1985.
8  Braun, Emily *Italian Art in the 20th Century*, Prestel, 1989.
9  Sottsass, Ettore 'Design and Theory', in *Design Since 1945* catalogue, Philadelphia Museum of Art, 1983, p. 3.
10  Hebdige, Dick *Hiding in the Light*, Routledge, 1988, pp. 77–115. Hebdige has written what he calls a 'dossier' on the Italian motor scooter, which includes a spirited discussion about the gender of machinery.
11  Kennedy, Paul *op. cit.*, pp. 355–6.

## CHAPTER 3

1  Manzini, Ezio *The Material of Invention*, Arcadia, 1988, p. 131. This book is full of poetic insights: 'The domestication of fire that started so many thousands of years ago is now complete. The new hot domestic object no longer burns the finger.'
2  Gordon, J.E. *The New Science of Strong Materials*, Penguin, 1976, pp. 173–205. See also, Fiore, L. and Gianotti, G. 'Designing Matter', in *The Material of Invention op. cit.*

3   Mack, John 'Advanced Polymer Composites', in *Materials Edge* magazine, January 1988, pp. 17–23, and subsequent issues of this bi-monthly magazine published by Metal Bulletin Journals Ltd.

4   Waterman, Neil 'Materials for Profit', in *Engineering* magazine, January 1988, pp. 16–18.

5   Mack, John 'Advanced Polymer Composites' *op. cit.*

6   Mack, John 'Passion, Power and Polymers: improved materials in cars', in *Materials Edge* magazine, March/April 1988, pp. 33–42. The Treser–1 automobile is manufactured by a small company headed by Walter Treser, one of the founders of the Audi Quattro. The use of composites in the automobile industry is beginning to gather momentum. It is predicted (*Financial Times*, 23 August 1988, p. 12) that volume production of family cars using a substantial quantity of thermoplastics will begin in the early 1990s. The example under particular discussion is a prototype called 'The Vector' produced by GE Plastics – notable because it demonstrates that volume production is feasible but even more interesting because the thermoplastics used can be recycled: 'Body panels, having done a good job of shaping and protecting the car in their first life, can then be melted down, but with the material still retaining a large percentage of its original properties. So in its second life it could become, for example, a part of the car's interior trim.'

7   See also, Bloch, Robin *Advanced Composite Materials*, thesis submitted for the degree of Master of City Planning, Department of City and Regional Planning of the University of California, Berkeley, 1984. Bloch explores the connection between the development of new composites and the defence industry. He also traces the volatile nature of the industry. At the point he prepared his thesis the non-defence commercial prospects seemed doubtful, but the end of the 1980s saw a resurgence of investment.

8   Manzini, Ezio *The Material of Invention op. cit.*, p. 66.

9   Dawkins, Richard *The Blind Watchmaker*, Penguin, 1988; *The Selfish Gene*, Oxford University Press, 1976.

10  Harris, Myles 'Pygmalion Moulds a Mind: Computers and artificial intelligence', in *Spectator* magazine, 14 May 1988, pp. 9–12.

11  Harris *ibid.*

12  Gordon, J.E. *The New Science of Strong Materials op. cit.*

13  See Bellow, Saul *More Die of Heartbreak* (botany); McEwan, Ian *A Child in Time* (mathematics, physics); Stoppard, Tom *Hapgood* (small particle physics); and Updike, John *Roger's Version*.

CHAPTER 4

1   cf. Bloom, Allan *The Closing of the American Mind*, Simon and Schuster, 1987, pp. 75–7. Bloom describes his bewilderment that so much political, scientific and cultural effort is expended by great minds on great endeavours, yet the results, when translated into consumerism, are so tawdry.

2   Anon *A Further Notion or Two about Domestic Bliss*, 1870, cited by Hardyment, Christina *From Mangle to Microwave*, Polity Press, 1988, p. 1.

3   Hardyment, Christina *From Mangle to Microwave op. cit.*, pp. 1–19.

4   Scarry, Elaine *The Body in Pain*, Oxford University Press, 1985, in particular the chapter 'Pain and Imagining'.

5   The most imaginative explanation of the subjective element in the behaviour of small particles in physics is provided by the playwright Tom Stoppard in his play *Hapgood*, Faber, 1988. See also Hawking, Stephen W. *A Brief History of Time*, Bantam Press, 1988, pp. 53–61.

6   Tucker, William 'The Object', *Studio International* magazine, February 1973, pp. 66–9.

7   Freedman, Alix M. 'Forsaking the Black Box: Designers Wrap Products in Visual Metaphors', in *Wall Street Journal*, 21 April 1987. Robert Blaich, managing director of industrial design at Philips, is quoted by Freedman as having some of his ideas 'nixed' – a radio shaped like two African tom-toms was not accepted by the marketing staff. Blaich said to Freedman: 'The biggest risk isn't technological, it's psychological. We're still a very big company with a lot of conservative product managers.'

8   Larkin, Philip *Required Writing: Miscellaneous Pieces 1955–1982*, Faber and Faber, 1983, pp. 80–2.

9   For a novelist's interpretation of what a structuralist would do with 'Elaine', read David Lodge's *Nice Work*, Secker & Warburg, 1988. Lodge, a Professor of Literature and quite at home in the process of Deconstruction, gives a lucid and entertaining demonstration of the importance of getting a product name *right* on pp. 154–6. *Elaine* is manifestly wrong.

10  Stumpf, William 'Are metaphors enough to keep you warm on a cold winter's night?' Lecture delivered to the Icongrado/ICSID/IFI Congress on Design in Amsterdam, July 1987. Stumpf was concerned that a focus on visual imagery and metaphors can undermine functionality.

## CHAPTER 5

1   Reed, J.D. and Tynan, W. *Their Plates are Smashing, Time* magazine, 17 December 1984, p.90.

2   Lapham, Lewis H. *Money and Class in America: Notes and Observations on our civil religion*, Weidenfeld & Nicolson, 1988. He says he is interested in the 'cramped melancholy habitual among a citizenry that proclaims itself the happiest and freest ever to have bestrode the earth. Never in the history of the world have so many people been so rich; never in the history of the world have so many of those same people felt themselves so poor.'

3   See Duffy, Bruce *The World As I Found It*, a novel published by Secker & Warburg, 1988.

4   The Edinburgh Tapestry Company, also known as the Dovecot Studios, has its roots in a company established in 1912 by the 4th Marquess of Bute. It was influenced by William Morris's workshops at Merton Abbey, near Wimbledon, London, and the first two master craftsman of the Dovecot studios came from Merton Abbey.

5   Dormer, Peter 'Frank Stella Paintings as Tapestry', in *Apollo*, February 1989, p. 110. James More, director of the Edinburgh Company, puts the argument about the tapestry as furniture.

6  Dormer, Peter 'The New Advertising', in *Creative Review* magazine, December 1987, pp. 14–17. Through the judicious use of King Lear's (Shakespeare) 'Reason not the need' argument, the world-famous advertising agency Saatchi and Saatchi argued in their 1982 annual report that competitive advertising was probably the most efficient way of making design, good or bad, available to the public.

## CHAPTER 6

1  For a counter view, see Harrison, Charles *Abstract Expressionism II*, in *Studio International* magazine, February 1973, pp. 53–60.
2  Marx, Karl *Capital*, entry 593.
3  Baudrillard, Jean *The System of Objects* (1968), in *Selected Writings*, Polity Press, 1988, p. 12.
4  Paz, Octavio *Convergences*, Bloomsbury, 1987, pp. 50–67. Paz has an unashamedly romantic attitude to crafts. For example: 'The craftsman does not define himself in terms of either his nationality or his religion. He is not loyal to an idea or image but to a practice: his craft.'

## CHAPTER 7

1  See the documentation for the conference *Product Semantics*, University of Industrial Arts, Helsinki, 16–19 May 1989. Reinhart Butter is credited with designing the phrase 'product semantics'.
2  Montag, Warren 'What is at Stake in the Debate on Postmodernism?, in *Postmodernism and its Critics*, edited by E. Ann Kaplan, Verso, 1988. Montag captures the essence of postmodernist uncertainty when he says, 'We act within a specific conjuncture only to see that conjuncture transformed beneath our feet, perhaps by our intervention itself, but always in ways that ultimately escape our intention or control, thereby requiring new interventions *ad infinitum.*'
3  Scruton, Roger 'The Autonomous Institution', in *The Meaning of Conservatism*, Penguin, 1980, pp. 141–60.

# Illustration Acknowledgments

Photo Ed Barber pp. 27, 29, 31, 32, 154; Photo courtesy of the British Union for the Abolition of Vivisection (a wholly peaceful body!) pp. 14, 74; Fischer Fine Art Ltd, London p. 8; Courtesy of Horizon, photo Malcolm Hughes p. 122; Photo Andy Keate p. 21; Courtesy of the Yu Chee Chong Gallery, London, photo David Cripps p. 51; Courtesy of the Yu Chee Chong Gallery, London p. 79

# Index

# Index

# Index